MY EXTRAORDINARY LIFE

MY EXTRAORDINARY LIFE

MONICA SUCHA VICKERS

To order additional copies of this book, contact:
Xlibris Corporation
1-888-795-4274
www.Xlibris.com
Orders@Xlibris.com
115029

DEDICATION

I can fly higher than an eagle
'Cause you are the wind beneath my wings.
—Bette Midler

I dedicate this book to Grandma Sucha because without her, my life would be very different. She never wanted the spotlight or any accolades so I can hear her now, "Ach, I didn't do anything." I learned tolerance from her. She often said she learned tolerance from me. When I was older I realized how intuitive and wise she was and how she skillfully balanced a tightrope of letting me live while teaching me how to protect against injuries with devastating consequences. She is absolutely the person who instilled in me the confidence, determination and attitude that would be so vital in coping with a life with only one limb.

THANK YOU

I think a hero is an ordinary individual
who finds strength to persevere and endure
in spite of overwhelming obstacles.
—Christopher Reeve

Much has been said about the many obstacles I have overcome in my life, yet it wasn't all me. I had much support from family, friends, teachers, and classmates along the way. I sincerely thank you one and all.

Thank you to Pat Moreland Schoenfelder, my college roommate, who helped me gather the data for this book. She gave me the push I needed to complete it. We are, as they say, true BFFs.

Thank you to my parents who were given an incredible challenge at a very young age and yet moved forward with such improbable determination. It is hard for me to imagine what it must have been like for my parents to watch every day, many times helpless, as I learned to manage basic life skills. I wonder how many times they thought about what my future would be like. Mom was also widowed at a very, very young age. My dad died suddenly when he was thirty-eight. She was thirty-eight. I was seventeen. My six brothers and sisters were aged seven through fifteen. Faced with another life-altering event, Mom was again challenged with a daunting task of raising seven kids alone. Somewhere she found the strength and perseverance needed to move past such huge events. I might have inherited some of that. Thank you, Mom. I understand more than you know.

Thank you to my wonderful husband, Mike. He single-handedly restored and preserved my faith that life is mostly fair and that true love can see beyond physical appearances. He taught me how to feel attractive and how to be confident in that attractiveness. He reminded me of the difference between the important things in life and the not so important. He always knew just when to help me and when not to. He made many of my dreams possible and fostered many more. He is a master innovator with endless ideas, all of which have made my journey easier. I love you, Mike.

Monica

TABLE OF CONTENTS

CHAPTER 1

MY BIRTH

God will never give you any problems that He thinks you can't solve.
—Og Mandino

MY MOM AND dad grew up together in the same small town and married right after high school. Mom proudly boasts that she "married the most handsome man in Leigh." It seemed like they had the world at their fingertips. My dad joined the Air Force and was stationed for a time in California. The letters they wrote back and forth truly showed they were in love with a promising future. They were very young, very happy, and thrilled about getting married. Almost immediately, they were expecting their first child. They could not have known that this child would change their world forever.

I was born on September 8, 1954, in Salina, Kansas, at the Air Force hospital. I weighed five pounds twelve ounces. There are very few details forthcoming of this critical moment, but I can envision a collective gasp for breath followed by several prolonged moments of painful silence. What happened? What had gone wrong? What had been missed? Questions by everyone—everyone, that is, but Mom who had no idea that things were far from normal. Quickly, the doctor regrouped and carried on as if things were normal. I was immediately whisked away, even before Mom saw me. The emotional toll of this moment can still shake me when I think about it. What an unexpected shock. This was the first and last time my dad was present in the delivery room even though he would have six more children.

My mom was told that there were "problems" with the birth and that it would be better if she did not see me. She was sent home quickly to spare her the grief of seeing other mothers with their newborns. She was told that I was probably blind and deaf and that my internal organs were "reversed." The doctors and nurses did not want her to get too attached because they did not expect me to survive.

Wedding picture, my parents, Alvin and Agnes Sucha, September 26, 1953.

My multiple physical deformities were apparent immediately. My right arm was gone above the elbow, and it had a belly button–like muscle on it. My left arm was completely normal. My left leg was missing at the hip, but there was a rudimentary foot attached. *Rudimentary* means "resembling." This appendage looked like a claw with a testicular-looking sac on the palm. Four "fingers" were curved inward as in a clenched fist. The shin portion of my right leg was attached at the hip. The thigh portion was missing entirely. The foot on this leg had a normal ankle but with only three toes.

For almost a week, Dad went every day to the hospital to see me. Mom was getting restless as the days wore on. It was difficult for her to process the idea that she had given birth, seen no baby, had no baby, and yet no baby had died. She asked to see me, and Dad took her to the hospital. "It wasn't as bad as I had imagined," she told me, describing her thoughts when she saw me for the first time. She did not believe I was blind or deaf despite what the doctors had told her. She is proud of the story that she shook a rattle over my head and was convinced that I could hear it and see it. She said she knew absolutely that I was not deaf or blind. It was perhaps a small victory—maybe things weren't as bad as first thought.

The doctors too were surprised that I was still alive; however, they continued to predict that I would not survive and most certainly would never walk. They advised my parents to place me in a home. I remained in the hospital until October 19. During that month, the Air Force helped my dad research various homes, including one in Boston. Boston—so far away from Kansas! Each facility had the same response—they could not accept me because my disability was not severe enough and/or they only took children with mental issues. Time was running out—I was ready to leave the hospital.

A huge decision lay in front of these nineteen-year-old newlyweds, and they turned to their parents for advice. Both sets of parents drove together from Nebraska to Kansas to see their new granddaughter and to help their children make this decision. When they saw me, I imagine they were also shocked and very saddened, but apparently everyone was masterful at keeping their inner thoughts quiet. Contributing to this was the fact that it was the Midwest with its very traditional values. Doctors were considered gods and their word gospel. Women usually kept their opinions silent. My parents and their families were very strict Catholics. Birth control and abortion were sins. Some even felt that my birth was a punishment from God for past bad deeds. Outwardly, however, they noted that I was cute, very tiny, and looked healthy.

Discussion of the options was held—find a home or take me home. Again, while not spoken aloud, they surely wondered how will clothes fit, how will a diaper fit? How will she crawl, sit up, or walk? Could there be mental issues as well? What kind of long-term care will she need, especially if there are other medical problems? How will we be able to afford it all? Will other kids make fun of her? Incredibly, no one spoke of these concerns. The decision came from an unexpected source. Grandpa Sucha was a tall, thin man who smoked a pipe and always wore blue overalls except for church. The skin on his face and on his arms below the elbow was deeply tanned and rough. He never said much about anything other than farming and the weather forecast, but he broke the deafening silence in the room when he quietly but firmly said, "If she were my daughter, I would take her home."

The answer suddenly seemed so simple: "I would take her home." No one ever looked back. A new and challenging journey for all of them, especially my two young parents, had just begun. No one could know then that they were just the right parents and grandparents to guide me to adulthood.

No one knows for sure what caused my physical defects. The medical records are missing. Thalidomide is highly suspected due to the type of deformities I have.

Thalidomide is a sedative, hypnotic, and antiemetic drug . . . used chiefly in Europe during the late 1950s and early 1960s especially to treat morning sickness but was soon withdrawn after being shown to cause serious malformations (as missing or severely shortened arms and legs) in infants born to mothers using it during the first trimester of pregnancy. (Merriam-Webster Dictionary).

The origins of thalidomide date back to the early 1950s in Germany by Chemie Grünenthal. They claimed that the drug would cure a lot of things, including morning sickness in pregnant women. They also claimed it would not harm a growing fetus. Both claims would turn out to be very wrong.

The Food and Drug Administration of the United States never approved thalidomide for general use. However, it is believed that it was distributed in the United States as part of a clinical testing program or obtained from other countries. Eventually the tragic effects of thalidomide began to surface. It affected boys the same as girls, often with limb deformity, shortening or absence. It is unknown how many worldwide victims there are, but the number would have been much greater in the United States had it been approved for use.

Makes me wonder—was I chosen, or just lucky?

Medical records for Mom's pregnancy with me are available, but some of the notes are missing. There is brief mention of a kidney infection, but nothing about a hospitalization or any treatment. Mom remembers specifically being hospitalized during her early pregnancy. She remembers being given only one pill though she does not recall for what. She is convinced, however, that the correlation between that one pill and my birth defects is not coincidental. From the moment I was born until she was almost seventy-five years old, she quietly but steadfastly refused to take any other pill, including aspirin. She spent a lifetime wishing she could have that one swallow back.

Many times I have wondered how my parents made it through that challenging reality. I wondered if they ever asked, "Why me?"

Monica, age 1, sitting on Grandma's floor.

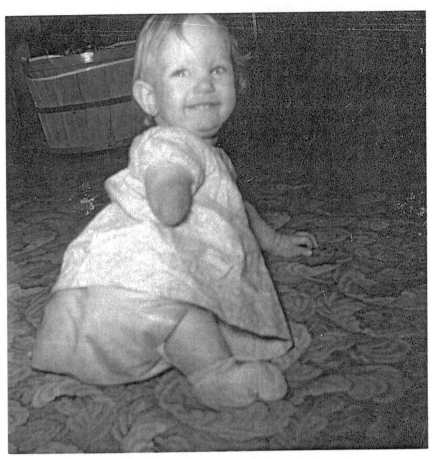

Monica, age 1. There is a pale green sock in my baby book
with a big hole in the heel. I went through a lot of socks.

MONICA SUCHA VICKERS

CHAPTER 2

THE FIRST FIVE YEARS

Where there's a will, there's a way.
—English proverb

SOON AFTER MY birth, Dad was scheduled for a military tour in Korea, but he never made it. Instead, the Air Force suggested that he take an honorable discharge. Apparently they felt it would be better for him to stay home with his wife and severely disabled newborn daughter. I am told the Air Force felt ill equipped to provide for my anticipated long-term continuing needs. I suspect also that this offer was financially driven, especially with the prospect of my predictable long-term disability needs. Dad accepted the honorable discharge in December 1954.

Also in December 1954, when I was three months old, my parents drove from Kansas to the Nebraska Orthopedic Hospital in Lincoln, Nebraska, for my first visit. They looked forward to this visit as they were very anxious about what could be done for me. There they met Dr. Fritz Teal. While I clearly posed a unique challenge, Dr. Teal was unwavering in his belief that I would be able to walk. He was a beacon in the dark and provided a ray of hope to my parents. An amputee himself, he asked my parents to return in six months.

In early 1955, my parents moved back to their hometown of Leigh, Nebraska. Dad was no longer in the service. They rented a farmhouse, and Dad farmed for one year. Very little is known about this time or what obstacles were faced by my parents and their families. Apparently, there was little to no discussion about how things were going with me. Mom and Dad also apparently did not initiate any discussion about how they were doing except perhaps privately to their mothers. There appears to have been a profound layer of silence wrapped around my birth, my deformities, my parents' emotions about me, and their efforts to figure out how to raise me as a normal child.

Family picture with Dad, Mom and 3-month-old Monica.

My first year of life was a true "trial-and-error" period. There was no instruction manual for raising a child with three missing limbs. Apparently everything was "normal." I was happy and healthy. From pictures, I can see that diapers somehow stayed on and clothes fit. Grandma Sucha made some of them. Mom said there were no issues with diapers or clothes.

Mom said they had no idea what I would do when they put me on the floor for the first time. Apparently, I moved around the floor quite quickly and easily and was undeterred by steps. One story is that Mom ran to snatch me off the steps as I began to climb them, but Dad held her back and said, "She has to learn." That would turn out to be a recurring theme throughout my life: "Try it first and if you can't do it, then ask for help."

Professional picture of Monica, age 1.

Sitting in a high chair waving hi.   Sitting in a high chair, different pose.

I do not have an independent recollection of that first year, but I apparently followed the usual milestones of crawling, sitting, climbing, etc. Mom told me that I always found a way no matter what situation arose. From entries in my baby book, I sat up alone at ten and a half months, I could recite the grace before meals within a week of hearing it, and I could sing fourteen songs before the age of three, including "Jingle Bells," "Walking in the Rain" and "Up on the Housetop."

The surprise of my birth had slowly given way to a flicker of hope—hope that things might not be as bad as first thought.

When I was seven months old, Mom was pregnant again. In a rare moment of raw emotion, she admitted that she was very frightened, anxious, and worried for the entire nine months. However, she is a very Catholic woman and categorically told me, "In my day, we took what we got. We did not have all the fancy tests of today."

In June 1955, my parents returned to the orthopedic hospital. I later found out that I was a guinea pig of sorts, and the planning began. The imagination, magic, and skill of Dr. Teal started to take shape.

My brother Mike was born in January 1956. Mom tearfully confessed that she was afraid to open her eyes and look at him. She kept asking the nurses if he had legs. Dad was not in the delivery room this time. Happily, Mike was a perfectly normal baby with two arms, two legs, ten fingers, and ten toes. The relief was palpable, not only for my parents but also for the entire family. Things were definitely looking up.

Monica and brother, Mike, playing on the floor. Late 1956.

The first year of farming was not successful. Therefore, my parents moved to Lincoln soon after Mike was born so Dad could attend college. He began college on the GI Bill and worked at a gas station six nights a week. The GI Bill was created in 1944 to provide benefits for returning World War II veterans. Some of the benefits included low-cost mortgages, loans, cash for tuition, and one year of unemployment compensation. It was available to every veteran who had been on active duty during the war years for at least ninety days and had not been dishonorably discharged.

Ten days before my second birthday, I was taken to the Missouri Valley Brace Shop in Omaha where the fitting and manufacturing process for my first artificial leg began. In March 1957, one month after the birth of my sister Barbara, the limb was ready. The "leg" was a just a nine-inch metal bar, which was the length of my real leg. The "foot" looked like a mannequin foot similar to those in a shoe store. However, my new "foot" sported a white sock folded neatly down and a white high-topped shoe with a brand-new white shoelace. It matched exactly the shoe, sock, and shoelace on my opposite real foot.

My left side without a limb sat in a bucket-like seat. There was a hole for my rudimentary foot. The seat with its "leg" was strapped around my waist, and I was stood on the floor. The room was very quiet and filled with doctors, therapists, nurses, my parents, and Dr. Teal. He reached down, took my hand,

and I walked with him. Suddenly, the room was filled with cheering and clapping. In that instant, the prediction that I would never walk was rejected. While Dr. Teal had been confident from the very first day, my parents now were also believers. There I was—two and a half years old and walking.

Monica's 3rd birthday with brother, Mike and sister, Barbara, September 8, 1957.

This artificial short leg functioned well with minor adjustments until I was nine years old. I had appointments at the orthopedic clinic with Dr. Teal every six months. He was a kindhearted man, very soothing and compassionate. His hands were soft and gentle, and he radiated much positive energy to everyone around him. With each visit, I grew more confident. As my body grew, his plans for future limbs began to take shape.

At about age four, an artificial arm was tried. My arm, off at the elbow, slipped into the arm socket. A harness went around my shoulder and buckled in the front. The hand was simply a hook designed only to grasp an object. I vaguely remember using this arm. It probably would have become quite useful; however, I evidently also used it as a weapon to hit the other kids so it was taken away before I had it for one year. It didn't make a difference—I was already quite proficient with only one arm.

At the age of twenty-two, I tried another artificial arm. It was extremely cosmetic with a beautiful hand with lifelike fingernails. Unfortunately, this arm was very awkward and not at all useful. In addition, I hit myself in the head a lot because I was not used to having an arm below the elbow. When I used my short arm, I was used to certain distances. Using my short arm with an extension from the elbow always hit me in the head. I tried to answer the phone with it once, but again, I was already too used to my arm being short. This would be the end of any artificial arm trial.

In July 1958, my sister Theresa was born. Two weeks later, Dad graduated from college with his business degree and began his career as an insurance salesman for Bankers Life Nebraska.

In September 1959, I turned five years old and was ready for kindergarten.

Dad's graduation from college. He is holding newborn Theresa.
Standing: Barbara, Mike, Monica (almost age 4).
August 1, 1958

Mom with Barbara, Monica, Mike and newborn Theresa. August 1, 1958.

Barbara, Monica, Mike, August 1, 1958.

Monica (3), Barbara (1), Mike (2) in the backyard swimming pool.

Monica in the pool.

CHAPTER 3

ELEMENTARY SCHOOL

I have a disability—yes that's true,
but all that really means is I may have to take
a slightly different path than you.
—Robert M. Hensel

I REMEMBER WELL my first day of kindergarten at Park School in Lincoln, Nebraska. This was, as it was called then, a "handicapped school" where the handicapped kids went. My parents enrolled me in this specialized school because it probably seemed like the perfect place—a special school for the handicapped. My parents were learning as they went.

Mom walked me to the front door in my new red dress. I remember entering the classroom and seeing lots of wheelchairs, braces, and crutches. My class included k through grade 8, all in one room. There were three teachers and one nurse. I have a vivid memory of the classroom, the hallway, and the bathroom, but I don't remember much else about my kindergarten year. I do remember that the "bus" for this school was actually a station wagon.

Station wagon transport to Park School.

Kindergarten, Park School, September 1959

1st grade, Park School, September 1960

In 1960, as I entered the first grade, Mom and Dad had their fifth child, Keith, born on Halloween. We were all dressed in our costumes and ready to go trick-or-treating, but suddenly Mom had to go to the hospital. We almost missed Halloween, but luckily a neighbor was available to take us. By the time we got home, we had a new brother.

I did not like Park School. I wondered why most of my classmates would not speak. It puzzled me why many of them drooled. It was difficult or impossible to talk with them. I also did not like that a nurse always had to come with me to the bathroom because I was able to go to the bathroom myself. Before too long, I told Dad that I didn't like the school and I didn't know why I was there because I could talk, I did not drool, and I could go to the bathroom by myself. I had no sense yet that I was not considered a "normal" child.

Dad apparently agreed because in 1961, I was enrolled in the second grade at Sacred Heart Catholic School in a "normal" classroom. The school was very large with lots of steps. Mom carried me up the entire huge flight and then back down at the end of the day. My classroom was on the second floor. I had the first desk in the first row. There was a huge blackboard behind the teacher's desk. There were many very straight rows of desks. I remember how "neat and orderly" the room was and how nice it looked when all the kids were sitting quietly in their desks. We had to sit for one whole minute at the beginning of the day, following lunch, and following each recess with our hands folded on the desk looking straight ahead at the teacher. I didn't care. This did not bother me. I was so excited to be there!

Part of the Catholic curriculum in the 1960s was attending church every morning. Being in the second grade, we studied to make our First Communion and confession. Virtually the entire year was focused on these events. We had many practice processions in the church—how we would walk and where we would sit. A boy and a girl were paired together, beginning with the shortest "couple." Even though I was the shortest girl, I was not part of the procession (I don't remember

2nd grade, Sacred Heart
School, September 1961

why) but rather came out from a side room directly to the front pew. I could not get onto the church seat myself, but the girl next to me helped me. We practiced this many times. It was a great day. We had a wonderful celebration at home. A four-generation picture was taken that day with me and my great-grandma, grandma, and dad and is proudly displayed in my home today.

My First Communion, April 29, 1962

First Communion picture #2, 1962.

4-generation picture, 1962. Great-grandma (Katie Thalken), Grandma (Agnes Sucha - same name as my mom), Dad (Alvin Sucha), and me.

It still had not occurred to me that I was different from the others despite the fact that I had to be carried up and down the enormous flight of steps in that school. I don't remember who all helped with these steps or the steps at the church or the steps on the bus, but I know I was very happy in this "normal" school.

Mom and Dad had their sixth child in 1961, my brother, David.

In 1962, I started third grade. Third and fourth grades were held in a small building with only a few steps. I loved that better than the building with all the steps. This building was across the street from the main school and so was the playground. I did not go to this playground often, but I don't remember why. While the teacher and kids were at recess, I practiced on the piano and learned to play several songs by ear. I played one every day for the class to sing as part of our afternoon prayer following the lunch recess. I loved playing the piano, but I remember distinctly wishing I had two hands because every song sounded so much better with two hands.

I also learned to play Christmas carols by ear on the piano on my grandma Herink's piano. No matter how good I became, I always wished I had the other hand. My aunt also had a piano, and I played on it when I visited her. Sometimes I would ask her to play a song or two just so I could hear the melody and harmony of two hands. She was awesome. My favorite one she played was "Thumbelina." In high school, I learned to play "These Boots Are Made for Walkin'," a song made famous by Nancy Sinatra. I would play one hand while my friend played the other. We were quite good together. I never pursued learning to play the piano because I was never satisfied with the music from just one hand. To this day, however, I do love piano music.

In 1963, I started fourth grade, my parents had their seventh child (Ken), and President John F. Kennedy was assassinated.

My parents now had seven kids—in nine years.

CHAPTER 4

MY FIRST ORTHOPEDIC SURGERY

The difference between can and cannot is only three letters—
Three letters that can shape your life's direction.
—Remez Sassonere

THE TIME HAD come to replace the artificial left leg I had worn since age three. Slight adjustments had been made as I grew, but I was now nine and in the fourth grade. I was still the same very short height (about three feet) with the rudimentary "foot" on the left side. This foot was not easy to cover up with clothes, and my arm almost reached the floor. Dr. Teal said it was time to increase my height, amputate the foot for better cosmesis, and create taller, more normal-looking legs with bendable knees. Easier said than done. Amputate—not a great option, but I was excited at the prospect of looking more normal. I was only nine so I truly had no idea what it would really involve or cost me.

To accomplish this, amputation of the rudimentary foot took place in March 1964. I remember only sketchy details of that lengthy hospitalization, surgery, physical therapy, cast fittings, the smell of fiberglass, and adjustment to my new limbs, which I called bendable stilts. I was in a ward with some fifteen other girls of similar age who were all there for orthopedic reasons. I was unable to sleep at all the night before the surgery. Much of the surgical "prep" such as shaving the area took place in the middle of the night. Breakfast came like any other morning, but I was not allowed to eat on the morning of the surgery. The wait seemed endless, and I was very frightened. I wished my mom and dad were there with me, but I was told they would be there when surgery was over.

Things were different then—there were very strict visiting hours, and exceptions were rarely made. In a ward of sixteen-plus girls in various stages of treatment—bathing, toileting, dressing, or therapy—visitors could not wander around at will.

Soon they came for me. I was placed on a large stretcher that was very hard and cold. I remember the other girls waving as I left, many having made the same journey. The trip to the operating room was long and terrifying. I watched the ceiling go by. Then I stared at the roof of the elevator. I can still smell the hydraulics. The elevator had two doors, both of which had to be manually opened and closed. I can still hear the outside door as it closed, followed by the second accordion-type door as it locked in place. The halls seemed endless and dark. I could hear no sound except the wheels turning on the hard gurney. We went up in the elevator, but it seemed like I was in the basement.

I remained in the hospital as my wound healed. My sense of balance was off with that foot gone. The nurses and therapists constantly reminded me to lie on my stomach so my spine would stay straight and my left side would not "curve upward." I wanted to sit but rather spent most of the time on my stomach. Also during this hospitalization, I was cast fitted for my new artificial limbs—taller limbs with bendable knees that would now be on the right and the left.

The unmistakable odor of artificial limb fabrication was always intense as one even neared the department. This smell lingered unabated during the entire casting process. As I lay on the table waiting for the casting to dry, I thought, "Wow, this place really stinks." This odor is difficult to describe. It is very pungent, similar to a strong hair permanent—definitely an odor all its own. Soon it was time to remove the cast. Everyone wore gray aprons covered with plaster. They had white plaster on their hands and face. I never liked the process of cutting off the cast because I feared the saw would slip and cut right through me. My prosthetist was very soft-spoken and reassuring, and of course, the saw never slipped.

Soon after, I was back in the prosthetic department getting my first look at my new legs. They were strapped on me. Wow—they were so heavy (approximately twelve to eighteen pounds each side). Now I had to stand up. I was helped off the table and . . . there I stood looking into a full-length mirror. Wow, I was taller than the exam table, and the floor was so far away. Silently I could not imagine how I would ever walk. How would I ever move these heavy things?

When the prosthetist was confident that the fit was right, I was taken to a room with a long rubber mat going from one end to the other. There were railings on both sides of this ramp and mirrors at either end. An attendant held on to a white sheet tied around my waist to prevent falling. The prosthetist clapped his hands as I took my first step. My new walking experience had begun.

I realized quickly that these limbs would be controlled by my upper body. My arms, shoulders, and waist had already gotten a workout. My armpits were already sore from the crutches. If I walked one leg after the other, I could easily move the right side forward for a step. However, it took a thrust of my body to move the left side. I also had to be sure that the knee locked in place after I moved the leg forward or the knee

A day at the orthopedic clinic.

would bend from the weight and I would fall. If I moved both legs together in a swing-through gait, I would be moving about thirty-plus pounds. It was definitely a workout.

My physical therapist and I spent an hour or more together each day as I learned how to walk on "bendable stilts" using crutches. I loved her. I couldn't wait to see her each day. She was soft-spoken, kind, patient, encouraging, and funny. She was always glad to see me. The crutch for my short arm had been modified with a leather band cinched up with a shoelace. With these new legs that bent at the knee, I also had to learn how to sit down, how to stand up from sitting, and how to get up if I fell. There was heavy focus on the gait style of right-leg/left-crutch together followed by left-leg/right-crutch together. Soon I was out of the therapy room and walking up and down the hallway with the therapist holding on to the white sheet tie.

It was late summer of 1964 before I was ready to go home. Once home, Mom and I continued this physical therapy in the living room. She used a similar white sheet tie and together we walked up and down the living floor, back and forth, back and forth. I got so bored and did not want to do this every day. I suspect that Mom didn't want to either. I did not get to Grandma's house this summer.

During this time, Mom babysat for two kids. Their daughter was the age of my sister, and we all had great times together. When her parents asked if she had fun with all those kids, she said, "You know what, Mom? That Monica doesn't have any legs, but you should see her go up those steps!"

With all my brothers and sisters and the kids Mom babysat, it seems like I always had occasion to play school or *Romper Room*, a popular preschool television program at the time. We would go to the huge front porch and dance or read or color. It wasn't as organized as all that sounds, but I did enjoy being the leader. Lots of kids can lead to lots of bumps and bruises, but Mom and Dad were unsympathetic if there was no blood. They would often say, "Is it bleeding? If not, then it's a long ways from the heart."

In September 1964, I started fifth grade with my new taller legs. I went from three feet to almost five feet tall. The ground still seemed so far away, and I was afraid of falling. My classroom was again back in the main building with the huge flight of stairs. There were even more stairs because now I was on the third floor. In addition, I now had longer, much heavier limbs and I was not as easy to carry. However, arrangements had been made by someone because there were always two classmates waiting for me at the top and bottom of the stairs. They lifted me by the arms and up or down we went. No one seemed bothered that they had to carry me up and down the stairs.

Unfortunately, these limbs had to come off when I went to the bathroom. Since I could not get them on myself when I was at school, I could not go to the bathroom all day. Some days this was incredibly difficult. Grandma Sucha made me special underwear that would snap open; however, this would never stay in the right place and/or the flap would open and fall in the toilet. Soon I was masterful at not needing the bathroom all day as it was the easiest solution. I learned just how much to drink and when not to drink. I always preferred to have the legs off. I couldn't wait to get home every day to shed them. Scooting on the floor and climbing up on things was so much easier. I used my one arm as one leg, and the rest of my body swung through. I could do this really fast, which was almost like running. At one point, I fashioned a "shoe" for my hand out of milk jug lids. My "shoes" were always new because our family of nine consumed a lot of milk!

In 1965, I started sixth grade, also on the third floor of the same building. In 1966, halfway through this school year, we moved from Lincoln to Syracuse where Dad sold insurance for Farm Bureau Nebraska.

Dad was a hardworking man in a time and place when men were men, women were women, and a handshake meant something. He took very

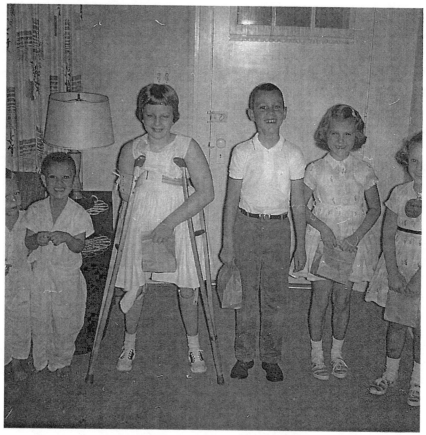

First day of 5th grade. David and Keith in pajamas.
Monica, Mike, Barbara, and Theresa. September 1965.

seriously his responsibility to provide for his family. My parents filled very traditional roles. It was Dad's responsibility to provide financially. It was Mom's responsibility to take care of the household and the kids, to prepare meals, do the shopping, buy the clothes, wash the clothes, taxi the kids to and from their activities and school, etc. Both of my parents worked very hard, and this work ethic was passed to each of us kids.

As an insurance salesman, Dad often worked late and got home after we were in bed. On the nights he was home, he insisted that we all kiss him good night before going to bed. It was our bedtime routine. I remember once not wanting to kiss him. I don't remember why, but I was a teenager so it could have been anything. He simply pointed to the space next to him and firmly said, "Get over here." When Dad spoke like that, it was pointless to argue. We could always have discussions about things, but in the end, he was the law.

My parents bought a huge kitchen table with nine chairs so that everyone could sit together at the table for meals. Sometimes Dad wasn't there and Mom was usually at the stove, but they were very proud that this table could seat all of us. Mom often told the story that in her family of nine kids, there were not enough chairs for everyone so some of the kids had to stand for meals. Our family's new table with nine chairs was indeed a big deal to my parents.

Dad was a die-hard Nebraska Cornhusker football fan. Well, okay . . . virtually every Nebraska resident is a die-hard Cornhusker fan. On Saturday afternoons, it was game time in our house, and there was only one television. Dad and Mike always got it for the game. Any of us could join them, but it was very, very risky to interrupt them.

For years, every time *The Wizard of Oz* was on, we watched it together. Mom made tons of popcorn, and we were allowed to eat it in the living room sitting on sheets. The lights were out, and it was like we had gone to a movie. I have fond memories of this rare "family movie night."

During elementary school, I never gave much thought that I was different from the others. My parents expected the same things from me as they did from the other kids. Virtually no allowances were made for me. I can still hear Dad say, "Try it first and if you can't do it, then ask for help." I learned at a young age that I would need to adapt to the world because the world was not going to adapt for me.

CHAPTER 5

SUMMERS WITH GRANDMA

100 years from now it will not matter
What my bank account was,
The type of house I lived in,
Or the kind of car I drove.
But the world may be different
Because I was important in the life of a child.
—Excerpt from *Within My Power* by Forest Witcraft

GRANDMA SUCHA WAS my dad's mother. She was about as tall as Grandpa, and she was full-figured. She had short hair, and she always wore an apron except to church. She had only half of her right ring and little fingers, the result of getting them stuck in the wringer of a washing machine when she was a young girl. My grandparents were married for sixty-five years.

Grandma had two children, Aunt Alice and my dad. She had eleven grandkids. My parents gave her seven of them. She had three grandsons before I was born. I was the first girl. The surprise and worry of my physical deformities was surely felt by everyone, but it was never discussed directly with me. I was much, much older when I began to ask, but I wish I could have discussed this with Grandma.

My grandma was the most loving, tolerant woman I have ever known. It did not matter your circumstances—she made you feel welcome in her home. She always had food to offer no matter the time of day. There was always a fresh, clean-smelling, soft bed to sleep in with feather pillows and a handmade quilt. Something was always baking. She was a true caregiver—whatever you needed, she was anxious to provide. She could anticipate your needs in advance. She was very religious but not preachy. She was a realist and applied pure common sense to all situations. She was trusting and saw the good in every person.

Grandma and Grandpa Sucha.

Grandma and Grandpa Sucha, dressed up.

When I was about eight, I started going to my grandparents' farm for the summer. Initially this began because my parents thought it was a good idea since the other kids were involved in sports, swimming lessons, and other physical activities. I couldn't wait to go. The summers were always too short.

There was an aura around Grandma and me. In retrospect, it was as if she was silently carrying a nagging heavy worry about what would happen to me when I was grown. She was eager to help me with everything, but she knew she could not because she had received the same strict directive from my dad: "Do not baby her. Let her try it—if she can't do it, then she will ask for assistance. Never assume she can't do something." I would sometimes notice that she held her breath, I guess from praying hard that I would not get hurt.

One of those breath-holding events was the tall flight of stairs to the upstairs three bedrooms. They were slippery and not wide enough for an adult foot. They were certainly not wide enough to sit on or climb. However, the steps never posed a problem to me or seemed dangerous. I could scoot up and down them very, very quickly. In fact, I simply slid down them many times, much like one slides down a railing. I could still hear Grandma's voice: "Monica, you be careful. No monkey business on the steps."

Grandma was skilled in knowing the difference between what she was afraid for me to do (and thus held her breath) and what she forbade me to do. For example, she allowed me to cut corn off the cob and shoot a BB gun, but I was absolutely forbidden to use a garbage disposal, put a spatula in a bowl with the mixer running, remove boiling water from the stove, take food out of the oven, use a butcher knife or even wash one, climb on the roof of the chicken coop, feed clothes through the wringer on her washer, feed an animal by hand, or put my hand anywhere near a fence with an animal on the other side. Still to this day, I am careful with knives, spatulas, and garbage disposals as if she is still looking over my shoulder. Grandma knew then what I know now—that I must remain vigilant in protecting my one hand.

I credit my grandma for saving the small belly button–like muscle at the end of my right arm (I have no elbow or lower arm). I found many, many useful ways to use this muscle. It is strong enough to hold lightweight things (paper, pencils, needle and thread, cigarettes, lipstick, nail polish brushes) and I have used it to buy minutes playing "Where did it go" with a restless baby. It had been suggested that this muscle be removed at my surgery in 1964, but my grandma voiced a strong opinion: "I think we ought to let her have what she was born with." I still have this muscle, and it is the sole reason

I can paint my own fingernails. If the lid is too big and I can't hold it, I put two-sided tape on the lid and then it won't fall out of the muscle. I have never had my fingernails painted professionally.

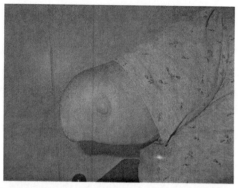

Picture of belly-button-like muscle on my right arm in the out position.

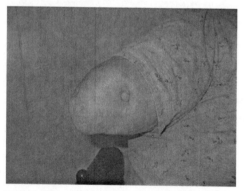

Picture of belly-button-like muscle on my right arm in the in position.

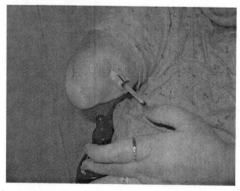

Picture of my right arm holding nail brush and painting my fingernails.

Frequently I would ride with Grandma to the cornfields where she would pick bushel after bushel of corn. She would search for and find just the right three or four ears with great golden silk and no worms so I could play doll with them as I waited in the car. Back down the hill, we would shuck corn for hours and get it ready for freezing. We always picked the best ears for supper.

Grandma also had marathon corn-freezing days. When the corn was ready, it needed to be picked. Delaying this process made the corn tougher and the kernels larger. I remember bushel after bushel on the front lawn. Usually there were many people helping. Even the youngest kids could shuck corn. Then it would be boiled, cut off the cob, and put in freezer bags. For our family of nine, Grandma made the bags extra large. Initially she did not want me to cut corn off the cob, but on this, I stood my ground and showed her how easy it was for me to do. I just put a towel down inside the pan and stood the cob on end. The towel prevented the cob from slipping. I could very easily hold the cob at the top with my short arm and cut down the side with my other arm. She allowed me to do it, and I was thrilled. These days were often ten-plus hours long, but I loved it. The corn was always so good to munch on throughout the day as well. If you can imagine a meal with a fresh chicken, fresh corn on the cob, fresh-made bread, fresh lettuce, beans, tomatoes, radishes, onions, and so on from the garden, you will then know the meaning of a feast.

I spent untold hours cutting "models" out of the huge department store catalogs, moms and dads and kids. I named them all. I dreamed a lot about what I would name my own kids. I sat them all in rows and played school with them. Grandma had a lot of huge catalogs from department stores.

She often let me bake cakes and make Jell-O and pudding. She never missed a chance to remind me not to stick the spatula or spoon into the bowl when the mixer was going. Grandma's house always smelled like fresh-baked something—bread, pie, cookies, cake, or something similar. The cookie jar was *never* empty. Bread dough was always rising under a towel, and I grew to anticipate the daily smell of freshly baked bread.

I washed a lot of lettuce. Grandma had a huge garden, and we had salad for every meal. I also washed beans and broke the ends off. I washed radishes, onions, strawberries, cucumbers, rhubarb, tomatoes, and celery. Grandma had a two-step stool that fit perfectly at the sink for these activities and also for washing dishes.

Grandma raised baby chickens and baby ducks. Oh my, they were so cute. I can remember the warm chicken house with the ceiling lights and feeders.

There were so many baby chicks chirping, walking over the feeders, and falling into the water. They were the perfect shade of yellow and were soft like cotton. Grandma always let me bring two or three in the house. I had a little home (a box) for them behind the kitchen door underneath the coat rack. I played with them and held them for hours. I changed the newspaper endlessly, but it never stayed clean for more than a minute. This frustrated me. It didn't take long before the baby chicks were too big for the house and they were returned to the chicken house. It was the same story for baby ducks.

Grandma also "dressed" chickens, and they ultimately went into the freezer. "Dressing" a chicken means killing it and getting it ready to eat or freeze. I remember so vividly Grandma catching a flapping, clucking chicken by one leg or two, and cutting off the head with an axe. I was amazed at how quick she was at doing this. Then the chickens were gathered up, dunked one by one into boiling water and then in cold water. This made it easy to pull out the feathers. At this point, the chicken was cut open and the insides removed. Finally, it was cut into familiar chicken pieces, placed in a bag, and frozen. I picked the feathers off countless chickens, and we had plenty of fresh chicken to eat. For a long time, I didn't even know you could buy a chicken at the grocery store.

I always preferred scooting around on the floor to wearing the artificial limbs. I always liked to sweep the floors (linoleum and hardwood) because I was "down there" and could see clearly when they were dusty. I also scrubbed a lot of floors from this vantage point.

A particularly fond memory of my grandparents is during a trip to the cellar during a tornado watch. Grandpa was trying to shut the cellar door against a mighty wind, but I was sitting in the way. That was because Grandma was sweeping the steps before I crawled down them. Every second was important, Grandpa was quickly getting nervous and Grandma was sweeping very fast. Noticing Grandpa's urgency, she calmly said, "Well now, Clyde, how would you like to scoot around in all this dirt?" Okay . . . now I sound spoiled.

I had a tricycle that I loved to ride. I stood up on my leg, swung my body over the seat, and pedaled using one foot. No problem at all. I would take it along to Grandma's for the summer. I loved that tricycle. I usually pretended I was a bus driver.

It still sounds incredible to me, but I totally enjoyed shooting a BB gun into the trees in Grandma's backyard. When I saw my older cousins using it, I wanted to learn too. Grandpa showed me the first time, but he was usually in the fields when I was "practicing." Grandma would carry and hold the gun until I was all settled into the red lawn chair and then hand it to me with strict instructions on where not to aim it. My wait for the unsuspecting bird began. When I found one, I would aim so carefully and shoot. Birds would scatter from the trees, but no bird ever fell so I guess I never got my target. But it was a lot of fun anyway.

I played baseball when my brothers, sisters, and cousins were there. I don't mind saying that I was quite good. Without my artificial limbs, I could very easily maneuver on the ground. My strike zone was on the ground, and I could hit the ball a mile without raising the bat off the ground. I was not the fastest runner, but to mitigate that, Grandma created a "fairness" rule. This meant that if I made it to base and then the next person behind me got a hit, they would be allowed to pass me on the bases, and if/when they scored, I scored. The fairness rule worked. Grandma had the best backyard for baseball. It was huge and fenced in. There was lots of beautifully mowed grass and strategically placed bases (an oak tree, the rhubarb patch, and the edge of the garden). She could often be heard cheering or offering pointers through the porch window.

I never liked my naturally curly hair. I wanted it straight. It was more popular that way. People even ironed their hair to straighten it. Each time I said this, Grandma would tell me that God knew exactly what he was doing because how would I be able to fix my own hair. With naturally curly hair, you don't have to do anything to it. She told me I should be thankful for it and that it was beautiful. I suspect that just to keep it curly, she often rolled my hair in curlers or gave me a perm. I still remember the smell of those perms (ugh).

I have always loved kids and babies. I was truly the happiest when I was rocking an infant or playing blocks on the floor with them. I could relate to being on the floor, feeling dwarfed when looking up at other people whether they were standing or sitting on chairs. And Grandma always said that I could comfort even the most distraught baby. I am told this started when my brother Mike and I were first separated. He was about seven months old and I was at Grandma's. Apparently, Mike would not stop crying until Mom and Dad had had enough and brought me back home.

During my summers at Grandma's, she made "play dates" with family and friends who had young children. This resulted in life-long friendships, good times and memories just as momentous as any other summer activity— memories that would surely have been missed if I had been doing the "usual and customary" summer activities.

One such life-long friendship is with my aunt who ended up having six kids. I remember being both nervous and excited the first time Grandma dropped me off at her house. She had just had her second child, and I could not wait to hold her.

I took my artificial limbs off quickly which I usually did because they were hot and not at all fun to wear. I got around by scooting on the floor and climbing up on furniture such as the couch, kitchen chairs, or bed. As my aunt and I were saying hello in the dining room, suddenly she bent down, handed me her baby, and asked me to change her. She said she had something on the stove and away she went. There I was—sitting on the floor with an infant, nowhere near a diaper, blanket, baby wipe, or anything. She yelled from the kitchen that the diapers were in her bedroom so away I went to change the baby. I tucked the baby on my shoulder between my neck and my short arm and scooted into the bedroom. I put her on the bed, pushed her to the middle, and then found the diapers. I got on the bed and changed her. It was really no big deal. I knew I could do it, but I didn't know how my aunt knew it. Blind confidence like this was certainly something I would not encounter very often.

Incidentally, the diapers at that time were cloth and held in place with pins. This was an enormous challenge in my life—getting a safety pin through a diaper without sticking the baby. I had no fingers to put underneath the diaper. I had to guess and pray that the baby did not move. I did stick one baby one time with a diaper pin. The baby was four months old and really cried hard. I picked him up to comfort him, the unpinned diaper fell off, and he peed on me so we were even. I felt awful and worse than he did. Happily, however, he loved me again within minutes. No one was more elated than I was with the invention of disposable diapers.

Grandma also had a very subtle way of teaching something that would be virtually impossible to ever forget. Take lying, for example. It was my job to wash the buckets of mulberries that had been picked. In case you don't know, eating or even touching mulberries causes significant purple staining to everything—clothing, fingers, skin, lips, teeth and so on.

On this summer day, just like many others, I was sitting on the step stool at the porch sink washing mulberries—very routine, I had done it often. On this day, however, Grandma asked me if I had eaten any. I said no. Why I said no is a mystery to me because that's what you did when you cleaned mulberries—you ate some. But for some reason on this day, I said no. Then she asked, "You wouldn't lie to your grandma now, would you?" I thought this was quite a silly question, and I was rather indignant as I again said no. She could hardly hold her laugh, but she was very serious as she pulled a hand mirror from behind her back and showed me my purple lips, teeth, and tongue. I can't even describe how I felt at that moment. Then in her typical grandma fashion, she said very quietly and lovingly, "There is never a reason to lie." Still today, I assume the answer is already known when someone asks me a question.

After I was grown and no longer spending the summers with Grandma, I realized that everything I touched turned to gold in her eyes. She started with an innocent presumption that it would be impossible for me to do much. Because of this, she was elated with everything I did, no matter how small or insignificant. She taught me how to sew because she probably thought department stores would not carry anything I could wear. She bought a sewing machine with a knee pedal since I could not use a floor treadle. We spent lots of time at the store in Clarkson choosing fabric and matching thread and zippers.

Once home, we would pin the pattern on the material, cut it out, sew the dress, and then I would wear it to church where she would proudly tell everyone that I had sewn it. Occasionally she would redo some of the stitching or redo the zipper. She thought I didn't know, but I did. She did not want to tell me that it had to be done over—she just did it. Her stitching was always very straight. Mine wasn't at first, but soon she didn't need to redo it. My right hand "muscle" (the one considered for amputation) could easily hold a needle that made it possible for me to thread it and subsequently tie a knot in the end. She cleverly came up with ways to sew on a button with one hand, letting me believe that's how it was done by everyone, not that she modified it for me. She gave me the sewing machine I learned on, and I still proudly use it in in my home today.

She taught me how to do embroidery, and I still love doing this. We made countless dresses and pillowcases. Through the years, I cross-stitched many baby blankets for my family and friends.

Sometimes, Grandma, Grandpa, and I would travel to Schuyler, a much larger town than Clarkson. When I was about eight, we went to a Ben Franklin five-and-ten-cent store in Schuyler. It was huge. While we shopped, I found a doll that I wanted. I asked Grandma if I could have that doll. She asked me why that one since I had so many dolls at home. I said it was because she had lots of clothes. Grandma said no but promised she would make clothes for the dolls at home. I knew she would so I never gave it another thought.

Quilt I cross-stitched for my friend who had twins, a boy and a girl.

Cross-stitched quilt, sample #2.

Cross-stitched quilt, sample #3.

Grandpa and I went to the car while Grandma paid the bill. Soon she came to the car with her packages, including the doll. She said the owner of the store, Mr. Brokenicky, told her that he wanted me to have the doll and he insisted that she take it. He told her that I was one of the happiest little girls he had ever seen despite my obvious physical problems. He was very touched by my attitude when I was told I could not have the doll. He also said he would like to see me every time we were in Schuyler. He requested that Grandma ask the staff to call him if he was not in the store when we arrived.

Of course, I loved the doll but knew nothing of the man or the conversation he had had with Grandma. At age eight, however, I wrote my very first thank-you note. The importance of thanking this man and any other person who gave me something or did something nice for me was stressed. As I sat down to write the note, I did not know what to say or even how to write a note, but Grandma helped me and we mailed it.

The next time I was in Schuyler and every time thereafter, I saw Mr. Brokenicky. He was an elderly man with slight tremors in his hands. He was usually dressed in a suit and tie. He was very soft-spoken. He was always elated to see me and genuinely interested in how I was doing. He always told me, "Pick out anything in this store that you want." As I grew older, it was uncomfortable to "pick anything I wanted." I told him I just wanted to see him and not choose anything, but he would have none of it. If I did not pick something, then he would pick for me. Eventually, he sold the store, but we remained good friends. For every holiday, even those not so significant, he would send me a card with money in it. Every time he sent anything, Mom made sure that I wrote a thank-you note in a timely fashion. This was never optional.

Most of my relationship with Mr. Brokenicky was via the mail, but he was always very encouraging in his notes to me. Most of all, I learned the value and necessity of thanking people for kindnesses or gifts.

When I was a senior in college, Mr. Brokenicky was killed in a car accident at the age of eighty-seven. When I attended his funeral, only then did I realize that his entire family knew about me. Many months later, I was mentioned in his will, which was very touching indeed.

I would not be the person I am today without my grandma, especially when you consider the other relationships I formed during my time with her. When the reality of my disability finally hit me, everything slowly came together. It was not a single defining moment, but rather a realization of the unwitting steps she took that prepared me for the emotional struggles to come. She had no plan to do this or any idea that she had made such an impact—she was just being my grandma.

Dear Monica:

Happy Valentine's Day! Hope it's a nice one too—weatherwise. With a few exceptions, it has been quite pleasant <u>this</u> year.

Pleases me that you like your University work, and life. "Write it on your heart that <u>every</u> day is the very first day of the year!"

Sincerely
F.J.

This Valentine's a lacy one,
With hearts
and flowers, too,
And somehow it reminded me
Especially of YOU!

Brokenicky

February 7, 1973

Valentine card and nice message from Mr. Brokenicky.

While there are many people and events that shaped my life, Grandma Sucha absolutely had the biggest impact, and yet she never knew that she was having an impact at all. I know I didn't. As the years passed, however, I realized that she knew then what I know now. I wrote her this letter in November 1995, thanking her for her indelible mark on my life.

Grandma died in 1998. At her funeral, I requested that the song "Wind beneath My Wings" be played.

She was, and still is, my hero.

November 1995

Dear Grandma,

I have been trying to write this letter for a while now. There are so many things I would like to say. Now that Thanksgiving is here, it seemed the perfect time to complete my thoughts. These thoughts are not new. I have carried them with me always, but it is only in the last couple of years that your impact on my life has been appreciated fully.

It will be 20 years in May 1996 that I moved to California. In looking back, it was undoubtedly one of my best decisions. The life I made for myself has truly been a happy one—much happier than had I remained in Nebraska. I needed a place where barriers were virtually non-existent. I needed to make changes that were initially very unpopular in Nebraska—the biggest one was giving up on the use of the artificial legs and using a wheelchair. This turned out to be the most liberating experience of my life. I have made a lot of changes like that one since moving here. California is so very different than Nebraska. Some of the adjustments were not easy, and sometimes the loneliness was great.

But I always felt that I could accomplish most anything I set out to do, and I owe this positive attitude mostly to you. My fondest memories are the ones I spent with you and Grandpa at the farm. You were always thoughtful, patient, kind, complimentary, encouraging and, most of all, not judgmental. You made me feel special and important to you. While I did not realize it during those summers I spent with you, those were the very qualities that gave me the strength to find my life in California. I thank you for that because this was truly the place I was supposed to be. I met Mike here, and my life has been deeply enriched by him as well.

My memories of you remain very vivid even though I have not seen you for many years. When I get lonesome, it is you I want to visit. When I sew or bake, I think of you. When I smell certain flowers, grass, alfalfa, or weeds, I tell Mike that my Grandma's farm smelled like this. When I see baby chickens or ducks at the fair, I think of the ones you allowed me to have in a box on the porch. I was always upset that they messed the newspaper so quickly. When I eat corn on the cob, it reminds me of the farm-grown corn, the husking, the canning, and the "puddle jumper" trips to the field. I remember ice cream after every meal, always my favorite cereal, my tricycle which I pretended was a bus, and the cookie jar always, always full that you heard **every** time it opened. And, I remember Clarkson, always a great trip!

I say this now because I want you to know the positive impact you had on my life. While we did not talk often, I always knew you were there—back home—always there. I knew I could talk to you any time about anything and that I would get an honest discussion, helpful hints, and advice but never an attitude of judgment.

I told Mike a lot about you and my memories of you. Both of his grandmothers are dead, and he has few good memories of them. He wonders what it is like to care about someone as much as I do you. He has had no such experience and says I am lucky because I have good memories that I can carry in my heart forever. No matter what changes, no matter how much time passes, no one can ever lessen the memories.

I had incredible sadness when I learned you were sick. I wanted to come home more than anything. As I struggled with the risks I would face in making a trip to Nebraska, Mike asked me a simple question, "Would your Grandma understand if you did not make it back?" I told him that of all people you not only understood but have asked me absolutely not to take such risks. I also told Mike how badly I wanted to see you. In spirit, I would give my left arm to see you but you would most certainly be the first to point out the foolishness of that! Therefore, having made the decision that the risks are too high (and at your insistence), Mike asked if I would regret not seeing you. I can't answer that yet. In the meantime, we are searching the country for an accessible way to travel, and if one becomes available, we will be there.

At this Thanksgiving time, I want you to know that I am very grateful for the indelible mark you made on my life. It is always good to talk with you—I hang up with a smile. If you need anything, I hope you will let me know. That I can handle from California. I also hope you will remember that not a single day goes by that I don't think of you and thank God that I had the benefit of your goodness and wisdom for a lifetime. When Mike asked me one day to describe you, without hesitation I said, "She is the essence of goodness. You would love her."

Love you always,
Monica

~&

Did you ever know that you're my hero?
You're everything I wish I could be.
I can fly higher than the eagle
But you are the wind beneath my wings.
--Bette Midler

Looking back, there is no doubt that everything I accomplished surprised and delighted Grandma. Amid all of her silent inner doubts, she was, unequivocally, my biggest cheerleader and my biggest admirer. All the doubts she had about my forecasted life faded slowly, but it wasn't until I married Mike that she was at peace and truly believed that I would be okay. Her focus then shifted. She reminded me often to take good care of Mike, and she urged me to write a book about my life. She said I would know what to write about. This is that book.

CHAPTER 6

JUNIOR HIGH SCHOOL

Self-pity is our worst enemy and if we yield to it,
we can never do anything wise in this world.
—Helen Keller

SYRACUSE, NEBRASKA, IS a small town just southeast of Lincoln, a town where everybody knows everybody. We moved to a small house in town on Mohawk Street. I had my own room, sharing it only with a baby crib and my baby brother, Ken. Every morning before school, I would lie on the floor waiting for Mom to strap on my limbs and stand me up. I could not do this myself. Many times, Ken would be standing in his crib smiling down at me on the floor. He was so cute in his diaper and rubber pants. He was also waiting for Mom.

As I waited on the floor, I learned quickly that it was no fun waiting for someone to help me. I became more and more determined to find a way to do things for myself so I could do them in my own time and on my own schedule. As I lay there, I imagined having legs and not needing to strap them on. I wondered if real legs were heavy because artificial ones were quite heavy. I also wondered what it was like to run up and down stairs and not need people to lift me.

In early 1968, we moved to an acreage five miles outside of Syracuse. The house was bigger; it was a huge two-story farmhouse with a well, a garage, a barn, pastures, and lots of land for all of us to play. Mom planted a massive garden of cucumbers, radishes, onions, lettuce, spinach, tomatoes, potatoes, and strawberries. She canned tons and tons of pickles. All summer our house smelled like vinegar. She sold cucumbers to the local grocer. More than once, she bought the grocery stores out of vinegar. She also canned tomatoes and peaches. It was a regular assembly line in our kitchen. We had a cellar that was used both for food storage and as a storm shelter.

Our acreage required a lot of mowing. I wanted so badly to mow, but Dad emphatically said no. This stuck in my mind because he always expected that I do everything the other kids did. I asked him why I couldn't mow. He was afraid, he said, that I would fall and pull the mower down on top of me. So I just sat on the porch and watched. I still love the smell of freshly mowed grass.

Our home on the acreage in Syracuse, Nebraska.

The house had one giant step, but Dad converted this quickly into a porch with four small wide steps with a hand rail. From this porch, he poured a cement sidewalk all the way to the road where the bus stopped. This was the longest sidewalk I had ever seen. It was at least seventy-five feet long. It was also extra wide, making room for crutches and ensuring that they would not fall off the sides into the snow or mud. It was awesome!

He remodeled the entire first floor of the house. He made two bathrooms, the master bedroom, and a hallway out of one huge bedroom. On the other side of the kitchen, he made a bedroom for me out of the kitchen pantry. This room was very small. It was painted lavender with darker lavender carpet. There was one long, narrow window about eight inches wide with lavender and pink striped curtains. He built my dresser into the wall and above it was a large mirror. I had a small closet with sliding doors, a twin bed and a small nightstand. I pulled out the top dresser drawer and put the kitchen cutting board on it for a desk. I used a kitchen chair. It was a room fit for a queen!

The makeshift desk in my room.

I could scoot up the stairs to the second floor and scoot all over. It was fun up there. There were three bedrooms with two kids in each room. What a great view. I never told Mom or Dad that the boys often went out their windows onto the very steep roof. Fortunately, no one fell off.

We had a "ritual" at the acreage—one that all of us kids remember well. After church every Sunday, Mom would make pancakes and fried baloney for brunch. These were not ordinary pancakes. They were the size of her big cast-iron skillet, which meant she could cook only one at a time. While we called these the "big skinny pancakes," we later learned they had a fancy name—crepes. They were awesome with just the right amount of crispiness around the edges. Fried baloney made a perfect accompaniment.

Our family had nine people, so cooking this "brunch" took a long time. Mom stood there for close to two hours making one pancake at a time. Even turning over such a huge skinny pancake required a quick-flip skill that no one had but Mom. It was like an assembly line. She would make one, put it on a plate, someone would eat it, and soon there would be another one ready. Eventually, everyone had enough to eat. Mom always ate last and always made the entire batch of batter. If there were any left over, they made a perfect snack. They were just as good cold, rolled up and filled with sugar, jelly, or rhubarb. This ritual was observed every Sunday after church, and truly is a memory that justifies the saying, "Those were the 'good ol' days."

Mom also cooked breakfast for a large crowd when three to five couples would come home with them following a Saturday night dance. Mom and Dad went to many dances and provided many early morning breakfasts for their friends. I was the babysitter. They always left me with the instructions to have everyone in bed asleep with the house "spic and span" before they came home. Sounds easy enough. After all, I was a fairly skilled babysitter.

But we had the "three little boys"—Keith, David, and Kenny. At their oldest, they were eight and younger. They ran like a pack. As if signaled by some synchronized buzzer, the minute the door shut behind Mom and Dad, they unleashed their mayhem and would listen to no one. They seemed to so enjoy the chaos they caused. I often solicited help from my other brother Mike, but he was also ineffective.

By the time Mom and Dad got home, however, the three boys had worn themselves out and were sleeping peacefully in their beds. The house was spotless. It looked like I was the best babysitter ever. Mike and I talked to Mom and Dad about the unruly "three little boys," but they just told us we were doing a fine job.

I had one paying babysitting job for a family with one small boy. Though I did not know at the time, Dad apparently had hinted that they ask me to babysit. He convinced them that I was capable of watching their one-year-old boy. Soon they asked me. I was elated, but I was so very nervous. I knew I had to do a perfect job. I had a great time and did very well. I was the babysitter for this family even after they had their second boy. This was obviously more challenging, but I felt so good when I was with these kids. I took off my artificial legs and scooted around the floor. I had both kids asleep and my legs back on before the parents got home. I doubt I would have had this experience had my dad not set it up.

After the move to the acreage, we rode the bus to school. Mom lifted me on and off the bus morning and night. One time the bus driver, an elderly woman, helped me. She was not happy about this. Mom was late getting to the bus, and after waiting for a bit, the bus driver decided, in a huff, to help me off herself. I recognized for probably the first time the feeling of being burdensome—a realization that accommodating my needs may not always be done willingly. At that moment, I was beginning to see how my needs, limited though they may be, could affect others. I did not like this feeling and absolutely did not want to feel it again. My determination to be independent was forming.

The seventh, eighth, and ninth grades were on the second floor with two large flights and a shiny slippery-looking floor. I had the usual assistance for these steps—Mom, classmates, and now a janitor. Because of these stairs, I did not go to the lunchroom in the basement or out for recess. I ate my lunch at my desk and looked from the second-floor window at the playground below. From that vantage point, I could easily see the kids who were bullies, the kids who got picked on, the kids who were left out, the kids who directed the playground, and the kids who did exactly as they were told. I could feel their feelings no matter how hard they tried to hide them. I often knew the truth of a playground incident that was being explained to a teacher. I never said anything, but I knew when someone was lying. I took note of how someone looked and acted when they were lying.

When the class went out to lunch or recess, sometimes there was a test or some other important stuff left on the teacher's desk. I never wanted anyone to think I looked at that stuff so I never left my seat, never walked past the desk for any reason. I wanted no accusation of misconduct that I had looked at anything on the desk. In the back of my head, somewhere I knew that trust would be huge in my life.

Never leaving my desk for recess, lunch or PE got to be quite boring so one day I left with the class and went to the principal's office. There was a manual typewriter sitting outside her office, and I asked her if I could type on it. She said yes. I spent lots of lunch hours there and got extremely fast hunting and pecking—incredibly fast actually. I discovered that not only did I love to type but I was good at it too. I then asked Dad if I could use his typewriter from work to type my eighth-grade term paper on "weather." He brought it home and placed it on my "desk." I knew nothing of ergonomics, but I completed several school papers using Dad's typewriter. Suddenly, however, the principal became concerned that I might be "learning bad typing habits," so she no longer let me use her office typewriter. She said I would learn how to type correctly in the tenth grade, which was just around the corner. I wondered what else there was to learn though. I thought I already knew how to type.

I don't remember a single bad incident in junior high school. The kids always treated me well. I had little clue from them that I was different. I couldn't shake the bus incident though. As I entered high school, I was determined to do everything possible by myself.

In September 1969, I turned fifteen and entered the tenth grade.

CHAPTER 7

HIGH SCHOOL

*The person who sends out positive thoughts activates the world
around him and draws back to himself positive thoughts.*
—Norman Vincent Peale

SYRACUSE HIGH SCHOOL, green and white, the Rockets. I was so
excited and yet a little apprehensive. The school was split-level—the first-floor
entrance was at the front of the school, and the basement entrance was at the
back. It was not easy or feasible, however, to walk around from front to back.
You went in the door where you parked. Again, there were stairs. Lots of
stairs. The lunch room, the gymnasium, and the home economics classroom
were on the lower level. Everything else I needed was on the main floor.

Students usually took a typing class in the tenth grade. Still quite oblivious
to the fact that I was different, I registered for this class. I was confident that I
had a huge head start since I had had all that practice in the principal's office
in junior high. However, after five minutes, the teacher came to me and said,
"You are not going to be able to take this class so there is no reason to sit
through it." He was nice and almost apologetic but he was pretty sure that I
would not be able to type. He said I could go to the principal's office and wait
there for my next class. I got up and left. I did not think much of it. It made
sense really—sitting through the class would be stupid, especially since I was
quite proficient in the hunt-and-peck method.

At dinner that night, Dad asked how my first day of high school went.
I told him it was great except they told me I could not take typing. As if he
did not hear me, he said, "What! What do you mean you can't take typing?"
Silently, I thought, *Well, Dad . . . really . . . think about it. Typing takes two hands.*
Before I could answer, however, he said decisively, "Yes, you can type. There
is a book. They will order this book and they will teach you how to type." He
went on. "You will tell the principal this first thing tomorrow, and if you don't

tell him, then I will come to the school and tell him myself." He spoke in his "dead serious" tone so I knew he meant business. I quickly agreed, but I was actually thinking, *Please, please, don't come to the school.* I could already feel the embarrassment. I would have to take care of this myself.

In fact, there *was* a book called *Typing with the Left Hand.* Turned over to the other side, it was entitled *Typing with the Right Hand.* I often wondered how he knew that, but I suspect he did more research than any of us knew. It took about two weeks for the book to arrive, and I spent this time helping out in the library. When it arrived, my self-led typing class was held in the principal's office. My home row for the left hand was f-g-h-j. I type many words with just my little finger (*were, are, tree, saw, dear, cares, lip,* etc.). Each day I turned several more pages and learned several more keys. Letters turned into words, turned into sentences, paragraphs, and pages. I could see quite quickly that this actually was faster than my hunt-and-peck method. The principal gave me a one-minute timed writing every day.

Home row for one-handed typing (left hand) = f,g,h,j
4,r,f,v and all keys to the left – typed with pinkie finger
5,t,g,b – typed with ring finger
6,y,h,n – typed with middle finger
7,u,j,m and all to the right – typed with pointer finger

Two weeks later when I reached the same speed (34 wpm) as my class, I rejoined them. My name was added to the huge wall chart showing the typing speeds of my classmates. I was quite surprised to see that my speed was second highest in the class. Doris was faster than me. While I never achieved a timed writing higher than Doris, my average speed was over 110 words per minute on a manual typewriter by the end of the tenth grade. It never occurred to me that I had one hand and Doris had two. I don't think it occurred to her either. She was too busy trying to stay in the lead.

CHAPTER 8

MY SECOND ORTHOPEDIC SURGERY

God promises a safe landing, not a calm passage.
If God brings you to it, He will bring you through it.
—Author Unknown

I CONTINUED TO attend the orthopedic clinic every six months. Dr. Teal had retired in 1969, but his orthopedic clinic continued with new doctors and staff. The artificial limbs I received in the fourth grade had been modified only for growth and repair, and in March 1971, it was clear that a new pair of artificial limbs was necessary. The same design could either be repeated or a new design created. The doctors and therapists suggested another cosmetic surgery to remove my normal right foot so that I could wear a more normal-looking leg. My parents and I discussed this huge step many times, but it was clear that they would leave the ultimate decision to me.

I thought about this over and over and over. I certainly liked the cosmetic reason. I had begun to think about boys, and indeed looking more normal would be a good thing. On the other hand, I also knew how much I used my foot. It allowed me to stand, making things easier to reach. It allowed me to get in and out of the tub, on and off the toilet, in and out of bed, and on and off chairs, couches, etc. It allowed me to climb up and down stairs, to stand up and reach the sink. I used it a lot, and I was definitely torn in my decision. A decision had to be made, however, so I would be ready to begin my senior year of high school. Cosmesis won out.

It was June 30, 1971. Just like in 1964, I was in a ward with other girls of similar age, all there for orthopedic reasons. Again, I did not sleep at all the night before the surgery. Again, the wait seemed endless and I was very frightened. Again my parents had to wait until after the surgery to be with me. Again, I was placed on a large hard, cold stretcher. The trip to the operating room was absolute déjà vu. It was, after all, the same route. I can still smell and hear that hydraulic elevator to this very day.

My gurney was parked directly outside the operating room door. I was sedated but still aware of my surroundings. I had time again to wonder if I was doing the right thing to have my right foot removed. As I lay there in the hallway, I saw a blackboard listing the surgeries for that day. There were only two—the one currently in progress and mine. Mine said, "Sucha-Symes, left foot." I thought, *No no no . . . it's the right foot.* I looked around to tell someone, but there was no one around. Suddenly I felt incredibly alone and more frightened than ever. Soon the shiny silver doors to the operating room swung open and a nurse wheeled me into the operating room. I again tried to point out the discrepancy on the blackboard, but she barely responded. After all, I was just a sixteen-year-old sedated patient. Another truth was that I did not have a left foot so I was thinking they were likely to get it right.

One of the last pictures with my right foot.

The operating room was quite scary looking. It was totally "silver" in color—the walls, the floor, the table, the instruments, everything. I remember asking the doctor where they put the amputated limbs, and he said, "We place them in a jar and line the jars up on a shelf in the operating room." I remember thinking that I must be the very first amputation ever because I did not see a single jar or even a shelf for that matter. Again, I was sixteen and sedated. The next thing I remember is waking up in the recovery room. I quickly saw Mom and my elevated leg. My foot was gone.

What had I done? My foot was gone. I was on the verge of hysterics. My leg was wrapped in a huge round bandage and elevated on pillows. I totally freaked out. Mom was there with our friend Marla. I kept repeating, "What have I done, what have I done? It's gone!" It was a miserable day emotionally and physically. The amputated area hurt and throbbed intensely. I was unable to urinate, and this was painful. They kept bringing 7-Up and I kept drinking.

I thought I would explode before I finally urinated. It was dark outside when I left the recovery room and returned to the ward. I never imagined anything could hurt so much. In addition, I was consumed with intense regret.

Recovery from this cosmetic surgery was very, very long, much longer than I expected. Pain was the biggest issue because now, instead of having my foot to stand on, I had the round bottom of a cut bone. The ankle joint was still present. My heel was left intact, but it had been stretched over the ankle joint and sewn in place on the top side of my leg with thirteen stitches. This made it possible for me to stand up on my heel.

I could absolutely not bear weight or stand on this area without intense pain for almost two years. Getting on furniture, on the toilet, in and out of the tub, among other things, was very difficult, if not impossible for a very long time. I had a hard time putting my stump into the brace socket. The incision in front of my leg pushed against the front of the brace when moving the leg forward. Phantom pain (pain in a nonexistent appendage) was excruciating. This can also include an itch that cannot be scratched or a cramp that cannot be massaged. In addition, it felt like my three toes had been tightly sewn together, but I had no toes anymore. They said these were nerve endings. Pain also hindered therapy because I could not or would not place weight on my right leg. Because of this, it was easier to swing through the crutches with both legs at the same time. My therapist, doctors, and parents did not like that at all.

I stayed in the Nebraska Orthopedic Hospital until the end of August. I met some good friends while there, and we are still in touch today. After our surgeries, the girls and I were not sick. We remained in the hospital just for therapy so we had some good times. Specifically, one girl and I would go to the end of our beds, stretch out, and grab hands. When we pulled, our beds would come together with a clang. We thought it was so funny except we could not get the beds back. All the girls thought it was funny and kept an eye out for the nurse! We had one very crabby always-in-a-foul-mood nurse who would huff and puff with steam coming out her nose and her face beet red as she hurried to separate us and admonish the entire ward for not being asleep. I admit we did this mostly to bug her because she was so nasty to all of us. The other nurses also thought it was funny and quietly encouraged us, though they quickly disavowed any knowledge of our antics. I had this same nurse in 1964 also. Her mood was ugly then too.

I still have phantom pain today. This is a well-known phenomenon following amputations. My foot still cramps up and feels like my toes are tied together and I cannot spread them apart. Reaching down to scratch something that is not there is very odd.

CHAPTER 9

SENIOR YEAR 1971–72

*Things turn out the best for the people who
make the best of the way things turn out.*
—John Wooden

I STARTED MY senior year in late August 1971 with my new legs. My focus was now more on football games, basketball games, pep club, homecoming, prom, and working in the library. Regular meetings of the Future Homemakers of America, Future Business Leaders of America, and the National Honor Society kept me very busy. I took an office practicum class with the new Selectric typewriters, and I absolutely loved school. I won the Miss Spirit award in 1971, an honor presented on the football field by the pep club during homecoming.

In January 1972, my dad got a job promotion to district regional manager and we had to move from Syracuse to Norfolk, Nebraska, about three hours away. I had four months left of high school, and I was devastated. He already anticipated that and had made arrangements with the people who bought our acreage to let me stay with them until I graduated from high school. I was a bit anxious about this, but in the end, that's what we did. My family moved to Norfolk, and I stayed with this new family for four months. They had seven kids too, all younger than me. I got to keep my room off the kitchen. I missed my family and all that was familiar, but this new family really made me feel a part of theirs. They had a piano, and I played on it all the time. Their oldest daughter could play the piano and often would play the "other" hand for me. We soon mastered playing together "These Boots Are Made for Walkin'."

My dad came to get me for Easter. We had a great trip to Norfolk, and I was so anxious to see the new house. He talked a lot about his new job, and it was obvious that he liked it. He asked how I was doing in my temporary "home." I told him it was great, the family was very accepting of me, and I was looking forward to graduation, which was about six weeks away. We talked about college. I told him I had decided on the University of Nebraska–Lincoln. He said I would love it there. Soon we were home in Norfolk. I had a great tour of the house. Preparations were already underway for the Easter dinner on Sunday. I was very anxious to see my grandma and grandpa Sucha on Easter. It was Friday, March 31, 1972.

Easter Sunday, April 2, 1972, was a beautiful day. After church, our home was full of friends and family celebrating Easter. The day was enjoyable, and the hours went by quickly. Everyone was having a great time. Grandma and Grandpa Sucha were the last to leave that night. They were not gone very long before an ambulance was called to our home. Dad had suffered an apparent heart attack. I watched as they wheeled the gurney out of the house. We lived only three blocks from the hospital. Mom and my brother Mike went to the hospital behind the ambulance. Some of the younger boys were already asleep, but the rest of us waited nervously in the living room. Soon Mom and Mike returned with the dreaded news—Dad died twenty minutes after midnight of an acute myocardial infarction. It was April 3, 1972.

Mom, so adept at keeping her emotions at bay when handling difficult situations, went immediately into her now familiar "I can handle anything" mode. She began calling the family members who had just left our home. My grandparents were not even home yet. When they found out, they turned around and came right back. The shock and disbelief were mind numbing, yet there were the usual details to attend to—funeral, casket, gravesite, luncheon, insurance, bills, and raising seven kids. I was seventeen, Ken was seven. The impact of this stark reality consumed my consciousness for a very long time to come.

Family picture taken in 1971.
Back row: Dad, Mom, Mike.
Middle row: David, Barbara, Theresa, Monica.
Front row: Ken and Keith.

For our family, the earth's rotation changed direction at that moment. We were catapulted into a new, unfamiliar, and unbearably sad place. None of us had any idea what to do next, what would happen next. Surely we were not expected to carry this much pain.

Following the funeral, I returned to my temporary home in Syracuse and graduated from high school six weeks later. I made double certain that I walked and did not swing through my crutches when it was my turn to receive my diploma. Dad was not there for my graduation. I could hardly process that reality. I felt like I was outside my body watching myself graduate. I was in a daze, unsettled and anxious. Mom hosted a great graduation party but still everyone simply went through the necessary motions. No one knew really what to say. When emotions are this raw, there are no words.

Following graduation, I left the family I had been staying with and went home to Norfolk. It was just temporary until college started at the University of Nebraska in August. It was a very difficult summer. Everyone was struggling bitterly with Dad's death, but yet it was not discussed openly. The pattern of not discussing things obviously had strong roots.

In My Dad's Own Words

Prior to my dad's death, he was interviewed by the town newspaper (*Syracuse Journal-Democrat*). I am very fortunate to have this sprinkling of his own words to add to my book.

Excerpt from *Syracuse Journal-Democrat*, *Syracuse, Nebraska*:

"She isn't one to have idle time. She likes embroidery, paint-by-number, and she made her own Pep Club outfit. She likes children and babysitting is her special activity.

She is a normal teenager and we are pleased with what she has accomplished.

After her birth, I traveled all over the country trying to find a hospital where she could be treated. We ended up at Orthopedic Hospital in Lincoln which is one of the best of its kind in the nation.

I believe much of Monica's success is due to the work of Dr. Fritz Teal of Lincoln. While Monica was more or less a guinea pig for new techniques, it was through these efforts and the work of Dr. Teal that the artificial limbs were designed and equipped with devices which made it possible for her to get around with the aid of crutches. The experimental legs were provided to us at no cost.

When Monica was born, the doctors said she would never walk but Dr. Teal thought otherwise and instilled in her the thought that she could do anything she wanted to do.

Her ability to get around is a joy to behold yet she does have a few obstacles where she needs help. Worst are steps but so far she has found plenty of help from her friends at school. She also needs help getting on and off the school buses but other than this, I don't believe there is anything she can't do.

She even plays softball with her brothers and sisters. She takes off her legs while batting and that creates a very low strike zone."

The article said he smiled as he said this. He did have a very quick wit! I am sure he also winked.

CHAPTER 10

COLLEGE 1972–76

Life is not easy for any of us. But what of that?
We must have perseverance and above all confidence in ourselves.
We must believe that we are gifted for something,
And that this thing, at whatever cost, must be attained.
—Marie Curie

IN AUGUST 1972, I started college at the University of Nebraska–Lincoln—the Cornhuskers, crimson and cream, Go Big Red! I moved into Selleck Quadrangle, the dorm on campus closest to the classrooms. I had a season football ticket! Mom and Mike moved me into the dorm, but I was very apprehensive when they left me there—alone. I knew no one. Classes and the church were quite a distance away. This was far for me to walk. I reasoned that I would have to start early to church. There was little choice. I was on my own.

Getting to and from class turned out to be quite challenging because of steps and distance. Many of the classes were far away, not only from the dorm but from each other, and it was difficult to walk such a distance carrying books. This challenge was considerably greater, and many times impossible, when it snowed. Someone either helped me or I missed class. There were no other choices. I listened to the weather at night in order to anticipate whether there would be snow by morning. Sometimes I would get help to class but would have to wait in the building for hours for help back to the dorm. I already knew that the snow was not my friend. Crutch tips and shoes get wet from walking in the snow, and a slippery indoor floor was as treacherous as the snow and ice outside.

Incidentally, I do remember, very vividly, falling smack on the floor in front of my eighth-grade English class. I was late because of the time it took to navigate through the snow from the bus, climb the outdoor steps, be carried up the two flights of steps to my classroom, and walk slowly down the long hall with wet crutches. As I entered the room, everyone was seated and class instruction had begun. One crutch slipped and down I went. The teacher and some of the guys helped me up, but the embarrassment of that moment lingered for a long time.

Football student ticket, University of Nebraska.

University of Nebraska football stadium.

Many of the buildings where classes were held did not have a ramp or an elevator. I had to allow extra time to not only walk a great distance but also navigate the steps to each. I soon learned the location of each building, how far apart they were, and how many steps they each had. I had to accommodate all of these things when I signed up for my classes. Many times, I had to choose class times two or three hours apart just so I had enough time to get to them. This usually also meant that I had to start early in the day and go late into the afternoon. Steps have never been my friend, and there are lots of steps in the world.

My first roommate was Marleigh. She was a junior from New Jersey. She was nice to me on the surface when we first met, but I later learned that she had immediately requested a room transfer on the first day, citing that she did not want to room with me. Much later she admitted that she was afraid she would have to do things for me and she did not want to be a nursemaid. However, she could not receive such a transfer for three weeks, and after that time, she rescinded her request to move. We became very good friends in a very short time.

Marleigh was quite excited to take me out drinking on my eighteenth birthday (the legal drinking age in Nebraska at that time). A bunch of her friends went with us to "barhop." The drinks they put in front of me tasted like punch and were easy to drink. Too easy as it turned out. Back at the dorm, the room was spinning and the black-and-white octagon-patterned bathroom floor was moving. Scooting across this floor to the toilet made me very dizzy. Marleigh took good care of me, but I was not anxious to "barhop" again.

Barhopping was a favorite activity in college, and Marleigh often went out on the weekends. I spent some time planning a fitting birthday surprise for her twenty-first birthday. While she was out, my friends and I took the mattress off her bed and put it in the janitor's closet. We replaced it with a Kotex pad on her bed with a note that said, "I washed your mattress for your birthday but it shrunk." Turns out the joke was on me. The janitor's closet door locked when it shut and we could not retrieve her mattress until the next day. The janitor, Gerri, came immediately to our room early the next morning when she saw a mattress in her closet. She just knew I had something to do with it.

Marleigh would curl my hair. We exchanged clothes. We tried to study in the same room, but inevitably one of us would have to go to the lounge. We had "M&M" as our identifier on the door. Someone quickly wrote "peanut" underneath it.

Marleigh was the first person to say the words "hand controls" to me. She was very confident that I could indeed drive a car if it were specially equipped with hand controls. I was skeptical at first, but she was so absolutely sure that I knew I had to check it out. Again I wished Dad was around to help me with this.

I grew to love Marleigh. We remained great friends until her death in 1976. She worked at a special education school and was driving the van taking children home when she was hit by a drunk driver. None of the children were injured, but Marleigh died at the scene.

The dorm had many rooms on both sides of the hallway. On the first floor, there were two bathrooms. My room was closest to the bathroom because I had to scoot on the floor down the hall before reaching the bathroom. On my short arm, I carried a bucket which contained my shampoo, razor, soap and washcloths. There were three showers, four toilets and six sinks.

Gerri was determined to be my guardian. She was a feisty redhead, always happy and anxious to help with anything. Her laughter could be heard at great distances, and caused all who heard it to laugh too. She loved all of "her girls." It was Gerri who found just the right chair to put in the shower for me to sit on. I can still hear her explaining why there was a chair in the shower and why it must be left there. She stopped in almost daily to see if there was anything I needed. We remained friends long after college until her death some years later.

My First Car

At the end of my first year in college, I went home for the summer. I told Mom I needed a car, and I told her about hand controls. She was receptive, but cautious. Even I wondered how we would do this—buy a car, equip it with hand controls, and then see IF I could drive it, or equip a car, see if I could drive it, and then buy a different car and equip that one. I don't know if Mom consulted anyone about this, but in the end, she took quite an unexpected leap of faith and we went looking for a car. She relied heavily on my brother Mike to help her decide. She bought a 1973 orange Chevy Nova hatchback. It was beautiful and smelled so new! Someone drove it to Omaha (two hours away) for installation of the hand controls.

1972 Chevy Nova hatchback – my first car.

Hand controls must be placed in a vehicle that has an automatic shift. Similar to the shift handle used to put the car in park or drive, hand controls are operated with a shift-like arm on the opposite side of the shift and connected to the gas pedal and brake. These traditional pedals are still functional for anyone else to drive.

Handle (lever) for the hand controls in van.

Hand control attachments to brake and gas pedal.

Pushing the lever backward engages the brake. The harder and faster you push backward, the faster and harder the vehicle stops. Pushing the lever downward engages the gas. This downward direction must be gradual until the desired speed is achieved. Unless the vehicle is equipped with cruise control, you must keep your hand on this lever pushed to maintain the desired speed. To stop, you let the lever rise up and then push it backward. This is very quick, just like the time it takes to move your foot from the gas to the brake.

This lever also houses the horn, the cruise control, and a button for the bright/dim lights, all within reach using only your fingers.

Driving with hand controls pretty much takes the entire hand. To using the steering wheel too, I had a knob attached. This looked like a donut, and my short arm, off at the elbow, fit in it perfectly and operated the steering.

Emergency brake.

Spinner knob on the steering wheel.

Switch control box for moving the driver's seat.

Lift controls on the outside of the van.

Soon the modified orange Chevy Nova was in the driveway. The moment of truth had arrived. I had never before even started a car. I had never before used hand controls. I remember so well my first turn of that key. I took a huge deep breath. Behind our house was a vacant lot where, under the watchful eyes of Mom and our neighbor Ed, I practiced for days driving in huge circles.

Soon Ed announced that I was ready for the highway. I was feeling pretty comfortable in the vacant lot, but I got quite anxious quickly about the highway. Thankfully, the traffic was light. Ed had me do various things like stopping suddenly, picking up speed, and then slowing down, turning left and then right, getting off the highway to park, parallel parking, and backing up. We practiced like this for only a few days and then he said I was ready to get my driver's license from the DMV. I was both excited and petrified at the same time. The DMV had a lot of steps, but I don't remember how I got up or down them. I don't remember the written test or the driving test. I don't remember getting my picture taken. I do remember saying out loud, "I passed." My license was granted, but there was one stipulation—hand controls were mandatory. I would begin my sophomore year in college with my own car and a driver's license. I was so happy.

Being able to drive felt like the future had absolutely no limits.

At the end of the summer, I drove alone to college two hours away in my new orange Chevy Nova to begin my sophomore year in August 1973. This year, in addition to meal tickets, football tickets, student IDs, I would need a parking permit. Wow. My new roommate's name was Vicky. We had a great year together. I still had little clue that I was all that different from anyone else. Why would it occur to me? I was doing what everyone else was doing.

Now that I had a car, I really wanted a part-time job. I found a temporary one at Lincoln General Hospital as a discharge analysis clerk on the weekends.

Then they wanted me to cover a maternity leave during that summer so the job was full-time then. I was so excited. This was my first job. My first paycheck was less than $100 but I stared at it for weeks before I deposited it.

I had this job for three years. I was responsible for making sure each chart was in the proper order and complete with proper signatures. I filed cards in the massive card file. When things were quiet, I tried medical transcription—my first taste. I loved it and quickly knew this was the career for me. I loved the hospital atmosphere, the medical terminology, and the camaraderie of the physicians and staff. I had to wear a white uniform, and I was ecstatic to wear slacks. The surgery to amputate my foot finally paid a dividend.

When this job went full-time in the summer of my sophomore year, I got an apartment with another girl from the dorm. She was very popular with the guys, and it was not unusual for her to date a different guy every week. Intermittently, and especially around her, I would wonder why I was never asked for a date. It was slowly beginning to dawn on me that my appearance might be a huge factor.

One of the men she dated and dumped was a guy named Patrick, a very nice guy whom I thought was quite cute. He seemed genuinely heartbroken over her and spent many evenings in my dorm room lamenting over her. I wondered if I looked like a therapist. I wanted to shout that she never did like him and that maybe if he got out of his stupor, he could see that I did. But . . . Patrick came and went. It was becoming alarming to me that there might never be a guy who would find me attractive.

When my junior year of college began in August 1974, I moved back to my old room in the same dorm, Selleck Quadrangle, room 6121. I had a new roommate, Pat. She was very intuitive. She seemed to not notice my disabilities. We were simply friends, not caregiver and friend. She sometimes carried books or helped me navigate the many steps in some of my classes. We enjoyed each other's company and had a lot in common. We enjoyed listening to a blind student play the guitar. Many times we would sing with her and an audience would gather. We were even asked to sing at a dorm-mate's wedding. Nothing ever seemed like an obstacle. Pat and I could do anything together.

Following my junior year, Pat and I took a trip in my orange Chevy Nova hatchback. I had never been out of Nebraska (aside from my birth in Kansas), had never seen the mountains, and had never camped or slept in a tent. Pat, on the other hand, loved doing these things and couldn't wait to show me the Rocky Mountains.

Pat always saw the glass half full and soon I too believed that the memories made would far outweigh the logistics. We spent much time looking for campsites with a bathroom I could use. We were very resourceful. I would turn sideways in my chair and Pat would lift up the middle of the seat, thereby collapsing the chair just enough to squeeze it through the stall door and out again. It did not take very long before we had an established routine. Pat would set up the tent and unload the trunk. Inside the tent, I would pull things in and set up our sleeping bags, backpacks, and ice chest. When we left, I would repack everything, throw it out of the tent, and Pat would load the car. We really were quite efficient. We camped at KOAs or in the back of the car for most of our trip.

With no destination in mind, we started west toward Denver. In Colorado, we stayed with Pat's sister and toured the majestic Rocky Mountains. We went to several open-air theaters nestled in the mountains. We went so high that there was no vegetation of any kind. The air was so thin. I was afraid of heights, but not Pat.

We then went to Wyoming, Montana, Idaho, Utah, Colorado, and New Mexico. In Wyoming, we were on our way to Devil's Tower but got spooked and turned back. Montana's nickname Big Sky Country was perfect since the sky looked so massive and blue there. In Idaho, we stopped alongside a huge field of purple flowers because it was so beautiful. On top of a hill quite a distance away was an abandoned old house. Fearless Pat thought we should go see it. After a fashion, she got me and my chair to the top. What an escapade! In Utah, we drove past the Great Salt Lake, but surprisingly, Pat did not suggest that we go for a swim. Finally in Albuquerque, we came to a crossroads—turn west and continue to California, or turn east toward Texas and back home. We turned east and then went through Texas, Oklahoma, Kansas, and finally home to Nebraska.

One funny story I have to tell: During a particularly stormy tornado-ridden evening in Oklahoma, we stopped early and parked in a restaurant parking lot instead of looking for a campsite. The car was quite small for changing clothes, unpacking sleeping bags, and reaching the cooler. At one point, Pat was in the back trying to reach something on the floor in the front seat. She was leaned over the seat, stretching far to reach the floor. I was trying to not get kicked when suddenly the horn started shrieking. Pat was leaning on it and could not get off. She was somehow stuck. Our cover to camp quietly in a parking lot had been blown, and we started laughing hysterically. The horn had drawn a lot of attention to a pair of bright pink panties and flailing legs. We were prepared to call home for bail money.

It was a trip of a lifetime for us, and Pat and I still talk about it. Neither of us could have known it would be the trip that launched the rest of my life. I now realized there were other places to live—places without ice or snow. For the first time, I considered that there might be somewhere I could live independently. I spent my senior year in college formulating the beginning of my next stage in life, and it would not be in Nebraska.

In August 1975, I started my senior year in college. Marleigh and Vicky had graduated, and Pat had moved off campus to an apartment with several other girls. I had the same room (6121) all to myself this year, and I really liked it. By this time, my brother Mike and sister Barb were at the same college but in different dorms.

I knew now that I definitely wanted to work in a hospital. My passion had been to work in a neonatal nursery, but I recognized quickly that it was not very realistic. Even if logistically I could get through the classes, obstacles, and hiring bias, in the end I knew that parents, already concerned about their neonates, would be uncomfortable with me. A bad outcome would surely always trigger a catch-22 situation—could it have happened to anyone or was it due to a limitation of mine. It would be an impossible position for everyone, including me.

I loved medicine, and I loved typing so I began taking classes on anatomy, physiology, biology, medical terminology, and Greek and Latin suffixes, prefixes, and combining forms. I didn't know exactly what I would do with this knowledge, but I absolutely loved the classes.

My shorthand, typing and business classes, office procedures, and accounting were held on the third floor of the Teacher's College building and there was no elevator. Three times a week, I trudged up and down three huge flights of stairs, petrified with every step. It took close to an hour to go up and another hour to come down. I had to schedule other classes around the time it took to navigate the steps in each building. My biology and anatomy classes had similar flights of stairs. My political science building had an elevator, but it was the farthest away from my dorm so I had to allow ample time to walk there and back.

My class schedule each day had to be carefully planned out. Many times it would take six to eight hours to complete two to three hours of class time. I was already aware that steps were a huge obstacle in my life, but my time at college really reinforced the fact that I needed to conform to the world—it would not conform to me. Sometimes I felt like I didn't fit in either the "normal" world or the "disabled" world. It was quite a conundrum at times.

It was starting to concern me that I was a senior in college and yet to have my first date. I now understood that perhaps it might be hard to like someone who needed help with basic things like stairs and snow, so I decided to move to a place where I thought I could be completely independent. I was determined not to depend on anyone, especially my family, to help me. I wanted my siblings to live their own lives, not lives that centered around accommodating my needs. I knew I had to move away from Nebraska. I told my family that I was moving because I wanted to live in a place where it didn't snow. It wasn't entirely untrue.

That place would be California. Pat and I began planning our second trip.

CHAPTER 11

MOVE TO CALIFORNIA

*Of course, there is no formula for success except perhaps
an unconditional acceptance of life and what it brings.*
—Arthur Rubinstein

I GRADUATED FROM the University of Nebraska on May 8, 1976. I did not formally attend the graduation—there were so many graduates. Instead, Pat and I drove past the graduation ceremony in my orange Nova, pulling a U-Haul and heading for California.

We started out on much the same journey as the year before. This time we had a destination and a mission. I was moving to California. Pat would stay for the summer but then would return to Nebraska to finish her senior year at college. We went again through Colorado and the gorgeous Rockies and on to Utah. This time, we saw the majestic Mormon Temple. Unfortunately, trying to back out of a tight parking space with a U-Haul proved to be an indelible memory. We went on to Arizona and the Grand Canyon. We got there after dark and had no idea just how close we parked to the edge (they probably made some new rules because of us). The next day, we toured the Grand Canyon. We navigated some trails definitely not intended for a wheelchair. Going down some of these trails was more like a thrill ride and a test of Pat's arm strength. Did I mention that I don't like heights or thrill rides? Pat needed help once pushing me back *up* one of those trails. Yes—our limit had been reached. What great memories.

We were on the final leg of our journey—we crossed into California, heading west to the ocean. On the map, we thought "Oceanside" might be a great place to see the ocean, so that became our destination. Soon we were anticipating the ocean over every hill, but darkness fell before we got to Oceanside. We stopped at Burger King on Mission Avenue. As we rested and ate, we looked out the window and saw a huge brightly lit sign: San Diego to the left, Los Angeles to the right. We were in the big leagues now. My parents had friends in California but did not know where. We had their phone number so I called them. It was about 8:30 p.m. They were home. They lived in . . . Oceanside. Really? Pat and I felt led by the Almighty at that point. We bunked at their home until we found an apartment three weeks later.

We slept late that first day, but then we went to see the ocean. It took my breath away as we approached. No words were spoken as we sat in front of the Pacific Ocean. I kept thinking, *Wow—there is no more land. We can't drive any farther west.* I felt humbled in front of the vast body of water with its many shades of blue and massive waves with white foam gently hitting the shore. The sound was penetratingly peaceful. The smell was pleasingly clean. It was the perfect place to reflect on our journey and be thankful for our safety. We had seen incredible parts of America, and we knew we would carry forever the memories of the purple flower field, the Rocky Mountains, the Great Salt Lake, the Mormon Tabernacle, Pike's Peak, the Grand Canyon, and now the magnificent Pacific Ocean. Our trip was over, and we were ready for the next chapter.

CHAPTER 12

FINDING A JOB

Adversity causes some men to break; others to break records.
—William Arthur Ward

PAT AND I found an apartment and moved into it two to three weeks later. It was quite a distance from Oceanside, and I don't remember why we went so far away. It was a nice apartment with a pool, and soon we were settled. Now it was time to find a job. I had no way of knowing what roadblocks would be waiting for me. I was still confident that I could do everything like everyone else, but this would be my first encounter with the real world, people who did not know me, and attitudes I had not yet faced. I was totally unprepared for the bias, patronization, and even discrimination that would start immediately with my first interview.

My first interview was actually with an employment agency where qualifications are reviewed and job interviews are scheduled at places where you would be a good fit. I even wore my artificial limbs to this interview, probably having a hunch that it would be wise to do so. I got to the office, and the receptionist handed me the application. I filled it out and was ready for the five-minute typing test. I was anxious to take this test because I was so confident that I would do well.

Suddenly, however, as I approached the electric typewriter, the middle-aged receptionist quite loudly informed me (and the rest of the office) that the off/on key was located on the right. She also educated me on how to toggle the switch between the clearly printed words *on* and *off*. Really? Did she just tell me how to turn on a typewriter? I am here for the express reason of taking a typing test and she feels she must explain how to turn on a typewriter before I even sit down? This really rattled me. I sat down and carefully placed my crutches against the wall. The atmosphere had now become strained, and I couldn't wait to get out of that office.

The five-minute test seemed like an eternity, but finally it was over. I methodically stood up, got my crutches, took my test out of the typewriter, and rather dismissively laid it on the receptionist's desk. I did not stop walking, but I reassured her that I had shut off the typewriter. She asked me to wait while she graded the test, but I told her that I no longer wanted a job through her agency. I realized then that I wanted a job I could legitimately do well because I was qualified to do it. I did not want anything handed to me just because I was missing limbs.

Just as I reached the car, I saw the receptionist running—yes, running—through the parking lot waving what turned out to be my test. She had graded it and learned that I typed 124 words per minute with two errors. She was very visibly surprised and a bit tongue-tied as she asked me to reconsider signing with her agency. I told her that I was sorry but I simply could not do that now. She asked why and I told her how patronizing she had been and how belittled I felt. I told her that it was okay to assume that I could turn the machine on and off. She understood and apologized. Then in an improbable irony, she said, "Look for a job where you can sit all day and type, like a medical transcriptionist." I thanked her and drove away. When I got home, I looked in the classifieds for medical transcriptionist. Scripps Clinic and Research Foundation had an opening.

I scheduled an interview at Scripps Clinic the next day. The personnel office was in a trailer with steps, so we met in the transcription center that was located behind a partition in the cafeteria. There were only two people in the department at that time. I was qualified in typing, spelling, English, and medical terminology; however, I only had limited transcription experience when I had dabbled at it for fun in college. There was much discussion with the supervisor out of my presence, but soon they decided. They said they would hire me on a "trial" basis. They would "try me out," and if it did not work, then they would have to let me go. Also, this "trial" position would be paid at half the pay they had advertised, but I would get the full rate if I succeeded. I agreed to these conditions because I absolutely knew I could do the job.

June 21, 1976

As I entered the freeway to begin my first thirty-mile commute to work as a medical transcriptionist, I had a flash of panic. What had I done? Nebraska and everything familiar suddenly seemed so far away, and yet there was no turning back. I knew instinctively that I was in the right place.

Pat also found a job and stayed for the summer. Knowing she would be leaving in the fall, I had to find a way to live totally independently. This was simply not possible with my artificial limbs, so I opted to abandon them in exchange for an electric wheelchair and a van.

After a cursory appointment, the California Department of Rehabilitation determined that I was indeed eligible for an electric wheelchair and a van. The process for this was much abbreviated once they learned that I already had a job. By the end of that first summer, I had a job, a van, and an electric wheelchair. My orange Chevy Nova was driven back to Nebraska, Pat returned to college, and I moved to an apartment closer to work. I was now on my own.

CHAPTER 13

MY FIRST JOB

Attitude is a little thing that makes a big difference.
—Winston Churchill

SCRIPPS CLINIC AND Research Foundation (SCRF) is an extremely prestigious hospital with specialty clinics, a sports medicine center, and an active research program. It is located squarely on the coast of the Pacific Ocean. When I first started, the building was small and old (transcription center in the cafeteria). From my desk, I could see, hear, and smell the Pacific Ocean. Many lunch breaks were taken out on the lawn right on the ocean. It was surreal.

Shortly after I started, Scripps moved to a new location, still on the coast. Between the building and the Pacific Ocean now was a pristine golf course where the Andy Williams Open was frequently held. Through a west-facing office, the view was a striking velvety green carpet of manicured grass together with unique shades of blue water and blue sky. There was a sense of peace, serenity, and prestige that equaled the reputation of this remarkable place.

The transcription center was no longer in the cafeteria. It was on the second floor. I could see down to the first-floor lobby by looking over a short wall. Looking up from the lobby, one could see the medical records department and our transcription center. I had never seen such a magnificent place. I was bursting with pride that I was an employee.

Employees at Scripps had to undergo annual employment physicals. During my first physical, the doctor asked what happened to me. It was the first time I had even thought about it, and after a short pause, I told him I didn't know. He seemed quite surprised as he asked, "Don't you want to know?" My thoughts were racing, but soon I said, "Yes, I definitely want to know." He then asked me the year of my birth and I told him 1954. He said it was unquestionably thalidomide but that he would confirm this with the medical records.

July '76

Lunchtime on the beach at Scripps Clinic.

Thus began the process of requesting the medical records of Mom's pregnancy and my birth. I learned that the military hospital in Kansas where I was born had closed and all records had been sent to a central records storage facility. After a time, the records were located and sent to my doctor at Scripps. After his review, he told me that unfortunately, the records were incomplete. There seemed to be gaps in the record. There seemed to be missing information during the first trimester when Mom remembers taking that one pill. The records did indicate that she had a kidney infection, but there was no mention anywhere of how it was treated or even that it was treated. There were no records at all of the hospitalization Mom remembers occurred at that time.

Now my interest was really piqued. What had happened to me? According to my doctor, it was not uncommon for records to be "lost" during the thalidomide scandal of the 1950s. He was quite confident in his conviction that I was a victim of thalidomide although we would probably never know for sure.

Disappointed and a bit angry, I turned to the family doctor I had as a child. His letter back to me was kind. He remembered me well. He too stated that I was, no doubt, a thalidomide baby, but he had not investigated this. At this point, I couldn't help but wonder why no one tried to find answers to the cause of my physical deformities.

In only a short time, I passed the "trial period" of my employment and was now making the same wage as other new hires. In our new office, our Selectric typewriters were switched for "magnetic card" equipment and eventually to computers and better computers, and then better-yet computers. Soon we were paid "by the line" with bonuses for exceeding the minimum daily line count. I always typed more lines than required, so I always got the bonus. I made a great living. It was not unusual for me to have two thousand lines a day. The national average was one thousand, and it was no secret that I was doing the work of two people. I loved my work because it fulfilled my desire to work in a hospital. While I had wanted to work in a neonatal nursery, transcribing reports for that nursery was almost like being there. I knew it was probably as close as I could realistically get. I loved my job, and I was good at it.

A transcription job was perfectly suited for me. A medical transcriptionist (MT) sits all day at a computer and listens through a headset to a recording made by a hurried doctor and then types it into a legible medical record, paying particular attention to content, proper format, spelling, and punctuation. Speech recognition software has been introduced in recent years, but a qualified MT is still necessary for an accurate report.

An MT must be able to read their completed reports and notice any nonsensical text. My favorite over the years remains "baloney amputation." Indeed this is what the recording sounds like, but an MT must be alert enough to know that this is really "below-knee amputation." Expertise in the use of the computer and word expanders (shortcuts where typing two or three letters will expand into a word, phrase, or even paragraph) is needed. Effective research ability is also essential.

I loved my career. It was physically perfect for me to sit all day. I was up close and personal with medicine when typing a patient record. I learned something new every day. I had no hindrances in this job, and I loved being able to do something the exact same way as everyone else. Having only one hand and no legs did not impact this job in the slightest. I was consistently one of the best. With this job, the "playing field" had been equalized. I had everything everyone else had.

My supervisor at Scripps Clinic took me under her wing. During this training, the atmosphere became quite uncomfortable for me. Soon it was clear that I was great for her image. She often bragged about how wonderful she was to help a person like me. She acted as though any accomplishment or greatness of mine was a direct result of her involvement. The better I looked, the better she looked. Patronization—I hated it. It was at the top of my intolerance list, and I could hardly hold my tongue then or now. I felt so diminished.

I let her believe she was my savior, but I became more determined than ever to earn everything I ever got because I never wanted the perception that I had an unfair advantage just because of my physical condition. I was perfectly able to distinguish between what I couldn't do, what was not wise to do (neonatal nursery nurse), and what I absolutely could do because I had the education and skills. Still there were people who believed I was lucky or had an unfair advantage. An unfair advantage—that even sounds funny to me.

My confidence level was at its highest during these first years at Scripps Clinic. I truly felt like I knew our department like the back of my only hand. In addition, my college education had focused on hospital administration so I was also confident that I could supervise the department. That opportunity presented itself and I applied. A coworker who had been there only a very short time also applied. I had never been so confident of anything—I was the obvious choice.

My interview went well, and my supervisor appeared to agree. But I did not get the promotion. In a separate meeting that included my supervisor and a member of the administrative staff, they explained why. I had indeed been the obvious choice. I was an exceptional employee. My work was impeccable. My knowledge of the department was unmatched. My qualifications far exceeded the other applicant. They seemed hesitant to continue, but they finally said I did not get the position because they were apprehensive that my physical appearance would be a turn-off for future applicants.

I felt like I had been hit by a Mack truck. What? Really? Can you even say that? Something felt viscerally very wrong. I would not realize until much later that this was discrimination in its purest form, but at the moment I was bewildered and dazed. It was hard to respond, but I said I understood and yes, I even agreed with their logic! Quietly, however, I was wondering what lesson I had missed in my life. Should I have even applied for this job? Maybe I should not be working at all if my appearance was that detrimental. Would this be the reaction always in everything? I even felt foolish for being so confident. I absolutely never considered that what I looked like might be a factor. That innocence had just been obliterated. Maybe I should consider first that my looks are awful, maybe it's true, maybe that's what everybody thinks. My mind would not stop.

I finished my shift and drove home. For the first time, my physical appearance made me cry. I was devastated. This is not how it was supposed to work. I did all the right things. I had the right education. I passed all the tests. I competed on the same level as everyone else. There had been no concessions made for me whatsoever. In my condo alone that night, I cried myself to sleep. Though I did not realize it yet, my confidence level and outlook on the future had been profoundly damaged.

I had to shake it off quickly because I still had a job to do. I convinced myself that next time would be different, that I needed to stay at the top of my game and be ready for the next opportunity. I became even more committed and determined to be the best.

Not surprisingly I suppose, this new supervisor and I did not get along. I take some of the blame for this because my attitude toward her was undoubtedly acrimonious. However, this supervisor had issues with me beyond this one. I always felt that she did not like me, but since that sounded paranoid and third grade, I never addressed it with her. Years later, after we both were gone from the transcription center, I asked her why she never liked me. To my surprise, she chuckled and said, "Oh, Monica, I know. I'm sorry. I just could not accept the fact that you could type faster with one hand than I could with two." I was stunned at her honesty but offended at the same time as I recalled the many years of angst she had caused me.

I wondered if this would always be the reaction I received when I was better than someone else. "Real life" was beginning to show itself.

I was becoming quite familiar with, and even at times expecting, a reaction to my physical appearance that would initially overshadow anything else I had to offer. Many times, the initial reaction would fade quickly, but it is so true—the worst thing about a disability is that people see it before they see you. Sometimes it is all they see. Unfair and erroneous assumptions and judgments are made. I felt like I had to "prove" myself every day and with every new person I met. It was very, very tiresome to jump through this hoop, but I saw no viable alternative so I had to find a way to cope. On occasion, I would meet someone, and there was no hoop—it was as if they saw me first and then, oh by the way, you are missing limbs. I can count these people on my only hand.

During my employment at Scripps Clinic, I moved on from the transcription center and typed exclusively for the neurology department and the orthopedic surgery department. I also learned how to do billing, coding, and scheduling. I worked with the team of physicians of the San Diego Padres. I worked on the weekend when the entire team came in for their spring physical. I typed up every record. I loved it at Scripps.

My friend Pam and I were consummate fans of the Padres. We initially met through a mutual friend. An amputee herself, Pam introduced me to Amputees in Motion (AIM), a support group for amputees and their families. AIM held functions throughout the year including dinner dances in April and December and an annual picnic by the lake at Camp Pendleton.

We attended many regular season baseball games, including every one with a giveaway, like a beach towel, T-shirt, and cap, among various other fun souvenirs. Many of our mementos are in the original team colors of orange and brown before the colors changed to navy and white. To avoid traffic, Pam and I would go two or three hours early and stay until the parking lot was cleared out. We hung around for player autographs as they left the stadium. We sat in my van and listened intently to the pre and postgame shows.

Jack Murphy Stadium, then used for baseball, was quite accessible for the wheelchair user. For regular season games, we got great seats; however, the person who accompanied you had to sit in the row in front of the wheelchair row. This made it almost impossible to visit during the game. For the playoff games, we were seated in the outfield. One accompanying person could sit next to the wheelchair using an uncomfortable folding chair. If there was more than one in your party, they frequently could not sit near the wheelchair. No matter, Pam and I were a fixture at the Padres games!

Pam and I also went to every home game of the two playoff division series and World Series in 1984 (Detroit won) and 1998 (Yankees won). It was a tremendous experience etched on our souls forever. What fun times!

1984 World Series picture.

Cub-Busters T-shirt, 1984 League Championship Series.

Tiger-Tamers T-shirt, 1984 World Series.

Earlier in 1984, the Olympic torch went by Scripps Clinic. We all went out to watch.

Waiting for the Olympic torch runner and van.

1984 Olympic Torch Relay van.

In 1978, I moved again, this time to a condo in Encinitas, a suburb north of San Diego. I lived there alone for eleven years. The doors to the bedrooms and bathroom were a tight fit for my chair. I could just barely get through the two bedroom doors, but I could not get my chair into the bathroom at all.

As it happens, I had a very sturdy 3 x 3 x 3 foot wooden stool that I had been using as a bedside table. I placed this stool just inside the bathroom door. It had to be moved if the door was to shut, but it was just me so it caused no real trouble. I would then slide from my chair onto this stool. This put me directly in front of the sink and mirror. From there, I could slide onto the toilet. I then pulled the stool so it was in front of the toilet. I slid again onto the stool and then I could get into the tub. Remember, I could stand on my leg and was then able to reverse the process and get back in my chair.

Once on this stool, I could also lower myself to the floor, clean the toilet and tub, change the kitty litter, scrub the floor, and straighten the rugs.

I had no housekeeper. I did all my own cleaning. In fact, I loved to clean. I simply slid from my chair to the floor to do the scrubbing. When on the floor, I could stand briefly on my one short leg to get up on the bed to change the sheets or up on the couch to open the curtains. Dishes and towels were placed on the lower shelves, but again, I could stand in my chair if I needed to reach higher. I used the armrest to balance me while I stood.

The neighborhood had many latchkey kids, and I met many of them almost immediately. When I finally met the parents, most of them said they just had to come over because their kids would not stop talking about me. I was happy to keep a watchful eye over these kids for many years. They were great company. I always had help at the grocery store and was always greeted when I got home from work. On occasion, I would take some of the kids to Baskin-Robbins for ice cream. I babysat lots of kids on New Year's Eve. At midnight, they took my pots and pans outside and banged them together. Then we had hot chocolate. Most could barely make it to midnight (including me), but it is a fond memory now.

I lived near a home daycare and became great friends with its owner. She had four young children of her own, including twins. My favorite picture is of these twins greeting me one afternoon. I had to quickly grab the boy because he had climbed up the side of my chair. I worked from 6:00 a.m. to 2:00 p.m., and when I got home, we all went to the pool. Many fond memories were made in Encinitas.

Twins, John and Carolyn.

During my last seven years at Scripps, I had the beginnings of what would become my own business, typing at night at home for some doctor offices nearby. I started this on a Selectric typewriter in my second bedroom.

Typing on IBM Selectric typewriter.

Another view of typing with one hand.

Selectric typewriter and transcriber machine.

Short arm is used for the shift, return and backspace keys.

I had several great clients, and my "business" grew rapidly. Since the opportunity for advancement was remote at Scripps and because I was getting busier and busier at home, I left Scripps Clinic in 1988 after twelve years. It was truly a very sad day for me—I had envisioned working at Scripps forever. However, when I learned that I was at the top of my pay grade at $10.64 an hour, I realized I had to move on.

CHAPTER 14

MY HUSBAND, MIKE

Just remember—in the winter
Far beneath the bitter snows
Lies the seed that with the sun's love
In the spring becomes the rose.
—Bette Midler (lyrics taken from "The Rose")

I WAS TWENTY-FOUR years old when I met Mike Vickers on April 21, 1979. He lived in Los Angeles; I lived in San Diego. We met at an AIM dinner dance in Los Angeles. He was a driver and had picked up several people who could not drive themselves. I saw him across the room. He stood out because he was so tall (six feet four inches, I learned later) with gorgeous red hair. I didn't think he had seen me yet.

For me, it was love at first sight, but I quickly pushed it out of my consciousness. By this time, I had become quite sinister to the idea of ever meeting a man, let alone the man of my dreams. I was convinced that my physical state was too great to go unnoticed. At this point, I had no more illusions that my disability was simply an incidental detail. Rather, it was actually a heavy burden that I often wondered if I could continue to carry. After all, it had already altered my choice of career, prevented a promotion for which I was qualified, and at twenty-four I had still not had a real date. It was very difficult to stay optimistic.

To my surprise, the tall redhead asked if he could join our table of five. He was solo and reasoned that we needed one to fill our table of six. I couldn't believe my luck. There he was at our table. The dinner was great, and the conversation was lively. We learned that his name was Mike, he was a building engineer, and he lived in Los Angeles. He was also a photographer and took pictures of the AIM events throughout the year. I wondered if he had an amputation since this was, after all, an amputee club, but he said simply that he was a volunteer driver for those who needed a ride. I could tell right away that he was fun to be around.

As we moved to the dance room, he came with us. Good grief, I was exploding with joy. The tables at the dance floor were very small and could seat only two people. Soon Mike was sitting with me—just us, alone! I was reluctant to like him so I doubly reinforced the defensive walls around me, insulating me from getting too close and being heartbroken. I told him that he did not have to humor me by sitting with me, that he should go dance. He replied calmly, "I don't like to dance." I told him that I didn't want him doing something different just because I could not dance. He told me again he did not like to dance, that he was just the driver and photographer. With that out of the way, we went on to have a great time. The dance went on around us.

When the time came for him to leave, he asked if he could see me again. I was speechless initially, but I said, "Sure," even though I truly expected to never see him again. I knew I really liked him, but some painful encounters with reality were still fresh. Getting my hopes up was not an option. However, as my friends and I returned to San Diego, I thought about the night and the good time I had. Apparently, I was uncharacteristically quiet, and the women I rode with confessed that they too thought there was something in the air between Mike and me. I told them I didn't think so, but deep inside, I hoped they were right.

Mike did call about two weeks later and asked if he could come to San Diego and take me to dinner. I was quite surprised and very excited. He said it would take about two hours to get to my house. I had just enough time to shower and dress for my first real date. I was twenty-four.

Mike arrived as promised. He drove a silver Datsun 240-Z. Impressive. He shared with me the pictures he had taken at our dinner dance. He did great photography work, and I learned that he had a dark room in his home. I learned that he was a stationary engineer and head project manager for the construction of high-rise office buildings in Los Angeles and San Francisco. He seemed very intelligent. I was riveted to the descriptions of his work responsibilities, and I was very impressed at his knowledge. It seemed like he could fix anything—plumbing, mechanical, electrical, construction, everything. Playfully, I asked him if he could fix my wheelchair if it were to break. He quickly said yes—he never hesitated. He never qualified his answer either such as saying he could fix this but not that. I loved everything I was learning about him. As an added bonus, my cat seemed to like him, and she was very discriminating!

Mike in a suit before one of our dates.

Mike petting my cat just before our date.

Mike was absolutely wonderful, very attentive, genuine, romantic, and best of all, interested in me. I felt like a woman for the very first time in my life. To him, I was Monica the young woman, not a disabled person who needed assistance. He held doors open because he was a gentleman, not because he thought I could not open a door. What a refreshing experience. Amazingly, there was no awkward, erroneous first impression to squirm through. In Mike's company, I didn't have to prove anything or be the best at something. There were no stares, glares, or pity in his eyes. He didn't need or want accolades for taking an amputee on a date. I felt elevated to a place higher than I had ever been before. I liked it.

We had a wonderful evening. I hated to see him go. Before Mike got into his car for the long drive back to Los Angeles, he bent down quickly and kissed me. I was in a fog as I watched him get into his car. I heard him say that he would like to see me again if it was okay. I wanted to scream from the mountaintop that it was okay and tear down my walls, but I held back. I was sure the other shoe would fall. He was simply too good to be true.

Mike and I saw each other every weekend for almost a year. He drove to Encinitas or I drove to Los Angeles. We had some incredible dates and learned that we were very compatible with similar philosophies, beliefs, and goals. We visited almost every local tourist attraction, such as Disneyland, Seaworld, Balboa Park, Knotts Berry Farm, San Diego Zoo, and the Pacific Ocean. We walked many times on the Santa Monica Pier and the Oceanside Pier just listening to the ocean. We took a one-week vacation to Yosemite National Park. The weekends were always too short. Once in a while, I dared to wish he did not have to leave.

After a time, the question of sexual intimacy came up. Oh my goodness—he was knocking on every wall I had so carefully and deliberately crafted. There was no way I could imagine being naked in front of him. After continued rejections, Mike gently suggested that I let him know when I was ready. My initial thought was, *Ready? Are you serious? I will never be ready.* Public reaction to my appearance with clothes was tough enough.

In addition, I was beginning to have some nagging questions: Why would a seemingly normal guy with a great job, a great car, and a home of his own be interested in me? Why would he, or anyone for that matter, intentionally choose a person with three missing limbs? It was quite obvious he could date anyone he wanted. What was I missing? What was he hiding? I needed answers.

I told my family all about Mike and how I felt about him. They were cautiously happy for me but echoed many of my own concerns. Even Grandma said initially, "Be careful."

No matter how hard I waited to see a different side of Mike, I never saw one. I continued to ask him, "Why me?" He replied that he honestly didn't understand it either. He never planned to date a triple amputee, but he had never met anyone like me. He said he had no real explanation except that I was kind, intelligent, funny, generous, thoughtful, compassionate, trustworthy, honest, and…beautiful. *Beautiful.* No one ever called me that before. However, I was still not convinced that positive character traits compensated in any way for three missing limbs. I continued to ask the "why me" questions over and over and over again. He always simply said that he enjoyed my company, I made him feel loved and special but he offered no further explanation. His actions alone were starting to convince me that maybe we were falling in love. Ironically, although I didn't know it then, he was thinking *I* was too good to be true and he wondered why I would want him. It was obvious though, that we were getting in deeper and deeper.

The moment I thought would never come finally did. I was ready for intimacy. My first time making love was magical and mesmerizing. I was now totally convinced that this relationship was for the long term. This guy was genuine. He had finally convinced me that I was attractive, desirable, and beautiful. My confidence skyrocketed. I was falling fast and deeply in love. Mike was too. However, the road to our ultimate happiness was about to become rather bumpy.

Meeting Mike's Family

Our relationship had gone to the next level—Mike invited me to meet his parents. One Sunday afternoon, we joined his family for a picnic in the park. In attendance were his father, mother, brother, three sisters, a brother-in-law, and a seven-year-old nephew. Although everyone appeared friendly, I felt instant discomfort and intense scrutiny. Afterward, I learned that his parents would not and could not tolerate me as their son's girlfriend. Once out of my presence, they voiced their anxiety, questioned his judgment, and "forbade" him to see me again.

This was extremely difficult on Mike. We had already processed together that there might be complications from our dating, but he was not prepared for their extreme negative reaction. Based on this, he worried about his position as the building engineer responsible for the construction of high-rise office buildings. He became apprehensive that his employer would have a similar reaction and question his ability to make good judgments. Ultimately though, he worried most about the toll all of these reactions would have on me.

I knew Mike was struggling. He was not prepared for his parents' reaction, and it hurt him deeply. I explained that their reaction was not all that unusual, really. I told him that I was confident his parents would accept us and like me once they got to know me. As far as I was concerned, his job would pose no issue at all. Despite my efforts, however, Mike was not convinced. He began to withdraw. Our dates went to every other weekend and even longer.

Shortly afterward, Mike announced to me that he intended to never marry even though that subject had not yet come up between us. His focus had clearly shifted to protecting me from the prejudice he blamed himself for causing. The option to date around was proposed. He theorized that since I had limited experience in the dating field, I was rather unqualified to really know who or what I was looking for in a life partner. He was quite creative in his efforts to convince me that he had lost interest in us. I did not believe him—not for a minute.

In spite of his proclamation that he would never marry, Mike and I continued to see each other off and on for several more years. He no longer spoke of me to his parents, and they seemed satisfied that we had broken up. Unfortunately, however, Mike had also convinced himself that marrying me was not an option and he often reminded me to date other people. I saw no logic in this—his actions and his words were so different.

Still, Mike thought it best that we break up so I could move on and forget about him. So we did. I was miserable. Mike was miserable too, but he honestly believed that this was the best thing for both of us. I understood all too well that he alone had to come to terms with the reactions that his family and others would have about us. I also knew we were hopelessly in love, so I tried to remain optimistic that we would be together again.

During this particularly painful breakup, Mike's mom called me out of the blue. It had been many years since I saw her in the park. The call frightened me. She quickly got to the point and very deliberately asked if I knew what was wrong with Mike. She wondered if I knew why he had become so withdrawn and depressed and never visited his family anymore. My heart ached when I heard this. "Yes, I know the answer," I told her. Trying to hold back tears, I said, "Mike is withdrawn and depressed because we broke up. He believes this is necessary because of negative reactions to our relationship." Very matter-of-factly, his mom replied, "Yes. It is for the best. We can all accept you as Mike's friend, but we cannot accept you as Mike's wife." It was as if she didn't even hear me. I spoke a little louder, "If Mike and I are meant to be together, it will happen no matter who thinks what."

During the time we were apart, I took the opportunity to date around as Mike had insisted. It was the early 1980s, and I joined the free-loving crowd and became a bit "adventurous" in the dating world, but nothing came of any of these one-night stands. After all, I had no intention of dating other men. I did not want to date around. I would never understand how this sexual freedom could be helpful to my relationship with Mike. I did not desire anyone else. I told myself over and over that I had to be patient until he came to terms with the fact that he wanted me.

Though the issue of what others thought remained unresolved, Mike and I could not be separated very long. We got back together and continued to see each other without announcing it to anyone. We always had a great time. We talked on the phone almost nightly. However, if the subject of marriage came up, he persisted with his mantra that we would never get married. He finally asked what it would take to convince me of this. Very flippantly, I said, "You will either have to marry someone else or die." I was becoming quite impatient with his logic now. Decision time was here for him.

Incredibly, Mike's decision was to marry another woman he had known for exactly three months. He drove down from Los Angeles to tell me. This was one of the most difficult nights of my life. Later I learned it was very difficult for him as well.

He reasoned that this was the only solution, the only way for me to move forward and forget about 'us'. On some level, that was true—in my heart I knew our love was strong and that he truly believed this was the only way for us to move on. However, I wanted some answers. I was very angry and hurt and did not understand. I asked many questions in rapid succession, giving him little time to answer. "Why was this happening? Do you love her? How can you possibly know you want to marry her in such a short time? I thought you were never getting married!" Everything he said sounded so trite and he knew it. Finally, I blurted out the hard question because I needed the answer. "Is this person easier for your parents to look at or accept into the family?" With his head hung, he hesitated briefly before saying, "Yes." At least he was honest. I told him that was ludicrous and that he was making a huge mistake. On some level, he knew that too. Within the hour, he was on his way back to Los Angeles.

My world shattered. Everything I thought I knew was compromised. How could I have been so wrong? How could have I been so ignorant to think it was at all possible for me to find a husband? What else had I been ignorant in thinking? Devastation overwhelmed me.

Five weeks later, on New Year's Eve, Mike got married. Several compassionate friends came over and sat with me on this tumultuous day. Once the tears started, they would not stop. I cried until I absolutely could cry no more. My friends joined my pity party, listened all day to my epiphany about the unfairness of the world, how stupid I had been, why me, poor me, and on and on. Every few minutes, I would place myself in Mike's world and wonder what he was doing. My heart ached like it never had before.

Needless to say, my outlook on life took an abrupt downward turn. I no longer believed that my attempts to be "normal" mattered in the slightest or were worth any effort. After all, my missing limbs had already cost me a well-deserved promotion and the only man I had ever loved. I could not muster any more fortitude, strength, or determination to cope with ordinary daily struggles. My positive attitude had been gravely wounded. Pessimism was consuming me.

I thought about Mike every day, constantly. One day, I became obsessed with depressive thoughts during my drive down the Pacific coast. I envisioned driving into the ocean. I wondered if my van would get stuck in the sand. I wondered how long it would take for my van to sink. Was this suicidal ideation? I didn't care. Still a faint voice in my head kept nagging at me, "If you change your mind, how will you get back to shore?"

Just in case this dilemma presented itself again, I signed up for swimming lessons at the YMCA. I was so very deathly afraid of water, but I reasoned that for at least one hour a week, my focus would go from ruminating about Mike to making sure I didn't drown. It worked! I learned how to swim. The deep end, the shallow end, it didn't matter. I could not reach the bottom of the pool at any depth. I was sure I would never float, but I was wrong. It took a while to turn from front to back and then back to front, but eventually I got the hang of it. Swimming with one arm propelled me in a circle, and it took some time to use force that matched the shorter arm so that I would go forward.

I began to look forward to my swimming lesson and the one-hour break from the Mike heartache each week. Unfortunately, there were still many hours in the day.

Swimming picture #1.

Swimming picture #2.

Swimming picture #3.

Monica on the diving board.

Swimming with floaties in the beginning.

My first float.

Ready to get back into my chair after swimming.

Three months later, Mike called me. It was very late, and I was very shocked to hear his voice. I could not believe it was him. It brought back a familiar flood of memories and my heart physically hurt, but I quickly remembered the dreadful reality that he was married. He asked, "How are you?" I replied, "I'm awful but why do you want to know?" He said, "I just had to know if you were mad at me." I was surprised and thought his question was quite odd, but I answered, "I am not mad if you are truly in love with someone else. I am angry beyond description though, because I just don't believe you are. I still have no idea what happened with us." He did not respond. Then I asked, "It's one thirty in the morning. Why aren't you home with your new bride? Does she know you are calling me?" He said he was still at work and no, his wife did not know he was calling. I told him that he should go home and not call me again.

I received another unexpected call from Mike fifteen months later. He called on a particularly bad day when I had gone home sick (depressed) from work. I simply could not get him off my mind and just wanted to crawl in my bed. Within minutes of getting home, the phone rang. For a moment, I considered not answering it because, after all, no one knew I was home. But I did answer it and it was Mike. He said he could not stop thinking about me and asked if he could come down right then to see me. Competing thoughts collided in my head—this would technically be an affair, yet I knew also that I had to see him if I were to have any hope at all of getting over him. I needed to know if my feelings were the same as they had been almost two years ago, or if they just existed in my head? I had to know the answers, so I said yes.

Within two hours, Mike was at the door. Within seconds, it was very clear that absolutely nothing had changed. For both of us, it was as if we had never been apart. I wondered if my torment over this guy would ever end. When he left, I carefully emphasized that I would not be his mistress and that I would not see him again without divorce papers in one hand and a wedding ring in the other.

A year and a half later, Mike was divorced. Our relationship resumed where it left off. He quit his job as a building engineer and moved from Los Angeles to Encinitas into my condo with me. Soon after, I received my engagement ring. The words I waited so long to hear finally came: "Will you marry me?"

Mike and I got married in Las Vegas on October 2, 1989, one month after he proposed. At this point, we had known each other for eleven years. We had met each other's families. We were very confident that this was right. His family from California, mine from Nebraska, and several close friends were in attendance. We had a sensational day, ceremony, and a reception at the Steak House at Circus Circus. I was definitely queen for a day. One month later, we had a reception at our neighborhood clubhouse.

Wedding picture taken at The Steak House at Circus Circus. October 2, 1989.

Putting the ring on my finger at our wedding.

Me and my sister, Barbara, at my wedding.

Me, sister Barbara, and Mom at my wedding.

MONICA SUCHA VICKERS

Our first kiss as a married couple.

Our first picture as Mr. and Mrs.

Wedding cake.

Wedding cake kiss.

Mike's family and I bonded quite quickly, just like I knew we would. Their initial reaction was really not that much different from any other family facing the same circumstances.

In retrospect, all the experiences Mike and I went through, including his marriage and divorce, were necessary in order for us to realize that we just had to follow our hearts. We balance each other like no one else can—it simply took time to learn that we don't have to explain anything to anyone.

CHAPTER 15

MARRIED LIFE

Life consists not in playing good cards
but in playing those cards you hold well.
—Josh Billings

IN 1990, MIKE and I bought a home in Vista, California. I had always anticipated that looking at houses would be challenging. Then as luck would have it, we received a tip from friends that these homes needed little modification other than the four to six steps to get in. They were right! The home we chose was completely accessible on the inside. It was perfect! Building a ramp was no challenge for Mike. After escrow closed, he immediately began building a ramp in the garage. He had prepared a blueprint and a detailed scaled drawing for the ramp in front of the home and submitted it to the Homeowner's Association (HOA). We were so happy.

When I first arrived at our new home, I parked across the street, as there were No Parking signs on our side. Before I was even out of the van, a woman appeared on her porch in a bright pink nightgown, yelling frantically for me to move the van. Loudly, she repeated over and over that parking on the street was not allowed. My lift had not yet even reached the ground. I tried to say hello and introduce myself, but there was no point. Unfortunately, since there was also no other place for me to park, I had no choice but to walk away. She stopped shouting and retreated into her home when Mike came out to check on the ruckus.

Incredibly, this parking issue escalated for months. Eventually, Mike and I were tasked with going door to door to ask the neighbors on our street if they objected to moving the No Parking signs to the other side of the street, thereby allowing parking on our side. Many were quite surprised at the storm this issue had created and of course did not object. The City of Vista thus agreed to move the signs, which paved the way for me to park directly in front of our home.

Problem solved? Nope! The five-member board of directors, in concert with the agitated woman, now insisted that there were issues of unfairness—if I could park on the street, then everybody should be able to. They could not or would not make an exception. They also alleged that this privilege amounted to being given "an extra parcel of land." Unbelievably, they suggested that we move.

Concurrent with the parking issue was the ramp proposal in front of our home. Mike's beautiful scaled drawing of what the ramp would look like was rejected outright. They claimed it would be an eyesore. They urged first that we move. Short of that, they advised that we move the wall of the garage back several feet so the van would fit. When Mike said this would be impossible and that the garage was not tall enough anyway, they said, "You surely could see this home had steps. Why did you buy such a house?"

It was all I could do to keep myself composed. I felt like shouting as loud as I could. Was this board of directors really so unaware? I thought about the great contrast between the ignorance I was encountering in the perceived enlightened state of California compared to almost none in the perceived not-so-enlightened state of Nebraska. Soon I heard Mike speaking. He was calm, firm, and resolute as he emphatically announced that we would not be moving, we would not be moving the garage wall back, and he would begin building the front ramp. He was resolute in his knowledge of the disability laws. He cautioned the protestors to read up on the law and take note that no one can legally restrict my access to my home.

As promised, Mike began building the ramp in front of our house. HOA directors would stop by in their car or on foot almost every day. Our phone rang and rang in what amounted to harassment. We had been in our home almost six months. I was almost sure that that we had moved to the wrong place.

We finally contacted the Disability Division of the Department of Social Services in Sacramento. A representative was sent to our next HOA meeting. Following this very heated meeting, we had no further trouble with either the ramp or parking. Mike went on to complete a beautiful ramp that matched the house decor beautifully. He landscaped the yard with rock, built planters, and planted trees and shrubs. It looked like the ramp had been there all along.

During this ordeal, we met lots of great neighbors and friends in the community who were overwhelmingly supportive. Before long, the initial handful of surly people faded away. A new board was elected. Mike was asked to become a member of the architectural committee and the landscape committee, due in large part to the great-looking ramp. He agreed to do this for two years. After that, he was voted president of the HOA for four years. We had most definitely moved to the right neighborhood.

The ramp in the front of our home on Barley Drive in Vista, California.

I became chairperson of the social committee for seven years, a position I loved. With help and support from friends and neighbors, I orchestrated ten Halloween parties including games, prizes, candy bags, cupcakes, food, piñatas, straw searches, haunted houses, cake walks, face painting, and apple bobbing in addition to the ever-popular costume parade, street dance, and raffle. A neighbor was a DJ by trade and supplied awesome music and microphone announcements for the entire party. I always made about 150 cupcakes. We all would get together to frost them and also to fill candy bags. With the money raised, we bought something for the community such as lights for the night parties.

The social committee also planned and carried out Easter egg hunts, Christmas caroling, campouts in the park, swim parties, barbecues, and chili cook-offs. I was totally and completely in love with life. The neighborhood was full of awesome neighbors and tons of kids.

Halloween cupcake frosting/decorating time.

Decorated Halloween cupcakes ready for neighborhood party.

A Halloween gang of kids.

Halloween guests at our home.

During our time in Vista, when my nieces and nephews from Nebraska turned nine, I bought them a plane ticket and they flew alone (with an airline attendant) to spend a week with us. Nine seems so young now, but they were all anxious for their "turn." We spent a week hitting the hottest tourist attractions like Disneyland, Seaworld, and the Wild Animal Park. Riding up and down on my van lift was a great new adventure for all of them. I have many special memories of my week with each of them.

Mike worked at the Wild Animal Park doing maintenance for the food service department, and I had my own transcription business. Every weekday I had a two-hour round-trip commute to various doctors' offices to pick up and deliver my work. At one time, I was picking up and delivering work from twelve different offices. The work I picked up had to be returned the next day. I worked long hours, but I loved it. At one time I had several "employees." Some of them drove to my house and picked up their work, and some of them picked up and then delivered their work directly to the client.

I had this business for fifteen years. I had the opportunity to learn many different aspects of this business. I transcribed many articles that were eventually published in medical journals. I was the production and layout editor for two monthly journals published by one of my clients. These journals were sent worldwide by mail or fax so I learned zip codes, area codes, and country codes. I learned how to bill insurances and how to code. I designed and typed virtually all the patient education handouts. I loved this business, and it paid me well.

As Mike neared retirement and the probability of moving approached, it would no longer be possible to pick up this work. Therefore, I sold my business and began working for a large transcription service company. This allowed me to work from home no matter where we lived. It was nice to be rid of the two-hour commute too.

In 2003, we built a home in Pahrump, Nevada. We moved there when Mike retired in early 2004. He always wanted to live in the desert, and Pahrump seemed ideal. It is located fifty miles west of Las Vegas and about sixty miles east of Death Valley, California. It is hot in the summer and occasionally snows in the winter. Roosters crow in the mornings. Our home was surrounded by beautiful mountains, and the sunsets were absolutely breathtaking every night. I worked from home, and Mike worked part-time as an exterminator.

Our neighbor had two young daughters who attended the local elementary school. One day they invited me to their classroom Halloween party. Wow.

I had such experience with Halloween parties and was so anxious to go. I made cupcakes. Following this, I became an official volunteer following an obligatory background check and fingerprinting. The person doing the fingerprinting matter-of-factly commented that I should get a discounted price. It was a great comment that broke the ice in the office when I laughed at it. I joined the parent-teacher organization (PTO) and eventually became its president. We held many fundraisers, some of which have become annual events. We raised enough money from these events to purchase a beautiful lighted marquee, which was placed in front of the school. Box tops funded several class field trips each year.

We had planned to live in Pahrump for the rest of our days, but as we grew older, the toll of being so far away from family began to weigh heavily. With my disability, I knew we could not live in Nebraska. My limitations were increasing with time, and travel was becoming prohibitive. Because of this realization, among other things, we decided to move to Phoenix. Two of my brothers already lived there. Mom and my sister also agreed to move there, and I suddenly was very excited to live so close to my family again. This migration to Arizona was completed in 2009. While I am not fond of the hot weather or the bugs, I am so happy to be able to join family holiday celebrations, day-to-day life, and Mom's cooking.

CHAPTER 16

WHY WE HAD NO CHILDREN

You don't have the power to make life fair,
but you do have the power to make life joyful.
—Jonathan Lockwood

I GREW UP imagining that I would have lots of kids. I daydreamed about what I would name them. It never once occurred to me that I wouldn't have kids. After all, the realization that I had any limits at all was almost not present while growing up. However, as I grew and reached for more adult achievements, I was introduced, sometimes painfully, to the restrictions.

One of these limits involved not having kids. There was absolutely no physical reason why I couldn't. It was simply my own very private decision. Many have wondered why and Mike and I usually just said he did not want any, but the real reason was my own.

A doctor I worked with had a disabled wife. I never knew what her disability involved, but she had kind of a limp, dragging one leg behind the other and it was difficult for her to walk. Despite this, however, they were elated when she delivered their first son. She brought him to work often to see his dad. We all got to cuddle him. We knew that they had a live-in nanny to help care for him because her difficulty walking made it very precarious to carry him. She often told us stories of how the nanny brought her the baby or carried him from here to there for her. I remember thinking, "I don't want someone standing by just to carry my baby somewhere for me. I don't want a nanny taking care of my baby either."

As this child grew to ages two and three, she brought him to work in a very fancy stroller. He was never taken out of the stroller because she could not catch him if he predictably toddled off and got into things. The child looked very complacent sitting in his stroller, never squirmy or trying to escape. Again, I thought, "I don't want my kids growing up in a stroller or a playpen because I can't catch them or even pick them up if they fall." I felt sorry for the little boy.

Eventually, this couple had three children. It seemed to be working for them, but then one day we received news that she had fallen down the stairs while carrying her three-month-old son. She fell on top of him. She would explain later that she thought she could carry him safely. The infant sustained multiple broken bones and required a full body cast for weeks. The image of that tiny infant in a full body cast lying in a stroller changed abruptly the direction of my life.

At that precise moment I decided not to have children. I was not willing to take any chance at all of dropping them or causing them injury because of my disability. Quite unexpectedly, my mind began to flood with questions. How would I get a child in and out of a car seat and up and down on my lift? How would I hold them while using my hand to operate the lift or unlock the house door? How would I get them in and out of a stroller?

My close friends assured me that I would figure it out just like I did for everything else. I knew that was true, but I also realized how much help I would require during the early toddler years. While my mind was made up not to have kids, I left the door cracked a bit just in case a future husband wanted children. I would be very willing to have a child if my husband's highest priority was being a totally interactive dad who understood fully how much "hands-on" involvement would be required, especially in the younger years.

Shortly thereafter, I met Mike. Very early on, without any prior discussion, he told me that he was not interested in having kids. Since it would never be his "highest priority" therefore, I agreed that I did not want kids either.

Through the years, Mike saw how much I enjoyed kids, and he wondered if he was the reason that we had no kids. He began to worry that I would resent him one day. I told him that the decision not to have kids was mine and mine alone. I reassured him that while he could have talked me into it, he could not have talked me out of it.

It was the right decision for us.

CHAPTER 17

KIDS

If you want the truth, ask a child.
—Unknown

I LOVE KIDS—I have always loved kids. Kids have given me more joy than anything else in my life. Even when I was little, I remember sitting in a rocking chair at Grandma's house rocking infants and small children. I would sit for hours rocking them even after they fell asleep.

For a good part of my life, I was on the floor or was *very* short. I understood firsthand how big everything looked and how intimidating it was looking up at tall people and things.

Kids are genuine and honest. When they have a question, they ask. It is quite normal, if not predictable, for them to ask me, "What happened to your legs?" I have an answer for kids of all ages—an honest answer, and most kids understand it. I tell them, "God made me this way when I was a baby." Most every kid will pause briefly and then ask, "Why?" I answer this too: "I don't know why, but when I get to heaven, I am going to ask." This is usually all it takes. The kids get a satisfactory answer, and it is the truth. A four-year-old said to me once, "Maybe God just made a mistake." Well, who knows—maybe he did. What an innocent conclusion.

Unfortunately, some parents will whisk their child quickly away from me or try to divert their gaze, their attention, and their thoughts. This is, by far, more uncomfortable than the question itself. When this happens, it makes me feel diminished, like an object that needs an explanation. I feel bad for the kids who get treated by their parents as if they said or did something horribly wrong. After all, they did have a valid and reasonable question that should be answered, I believe, as honestly as possible.

When adults ask what happened to me, however, I am offended. I expect adults to have more etiquette than to ask a question that is none of their business. That kind of information is learned as friendships are formed and developed, not just because we are in the same grocery line. If that were true, I would just wear a sign.

An unforeseen benefit of my interaction with kids is that the young ones have not yet formed any biases of what I can do or not do. They simply act as if I can reach things, lift things, tie shoes, put hair in a ponytail, or push them in the swing. One memorable moment was when a two-year-old girl at the pool insisted that I tie her shoes. Lots of people were around, including her parents, but in vintage two-year-old fashion, she wanted me to tie her shoes that day. Now I *could* tie shoes, but I had to use my mouth so I didn't do it often and never in public. However, on this day for this little girl because she was so insistent and I had no good reason not to, I picked her up, sat her on the table, and tied her shoes—with my mouth. I stood her back on the ground, and she scurried off to play. There. Done. No questions. Wow!

Another time a young child reasoned that I should dress as an apple for Halloween. She told me this would be perfect since apples have no legs. I could wear a red dress and a green hat.

Kids would imitate me when clapping their hands. Many parents throughout the years told me that their kids hit their elbow instead of putting their hands together. It's cute and very touching. A ride up and down on my van lift, the ramp in front of the house, or in my chair with me was as good as any amusement park ride. As they got older, some even liked running the lift for me. I was glad to let them. It was sad for them, and for me, when they were too old to ride with me in my chair.

Niece, Lindsey, taking a ride with me in my chair.

Neighbor, Benjamin, chillaxin with me in my chair.

My niece, Nicki, on my van lift.

MONICA SUCHA VICKERS

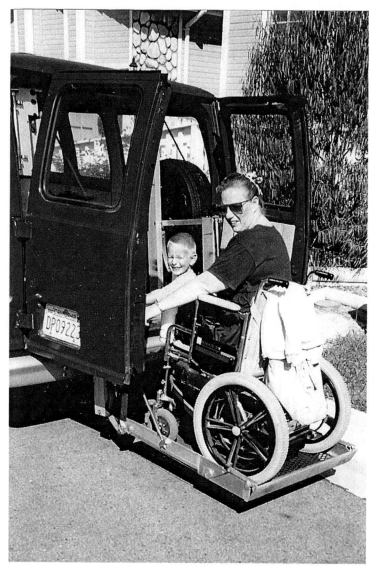

Nephew, A.J., and me on my van lift.

Neighbors, newborn Ben with Patrick, Sally and a blanket I sewed.

Niece, Nicki, in my chair with me on my van lift.

Niece, Jessica, on my van lift.

Nieces, Sara and Jessica, on my van lift.

Niece, Ellie, on my van lift.

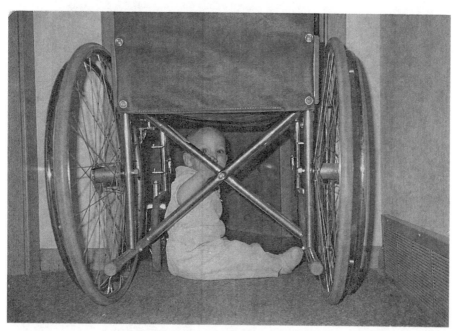

Niece, Sara, under my wheelchair.

Nephew, Stuart, too big to sit in my chair with me.

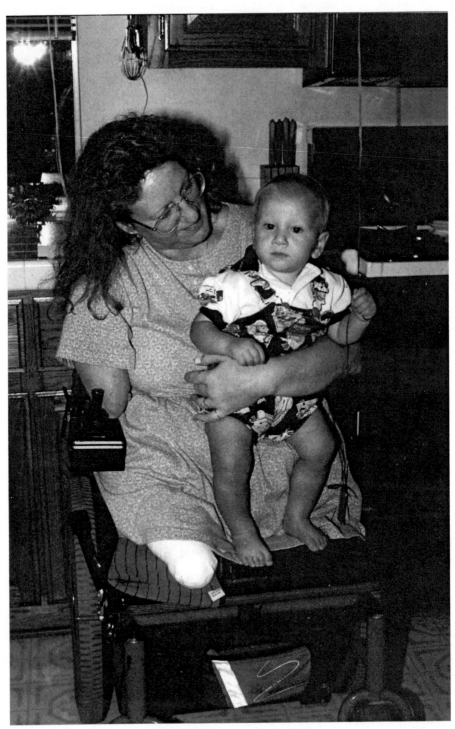

Neighbor, Peter, in my chair with me.

MONICA SUCHA VICKERS

Friends, Morgan, Jacob, and Madison.

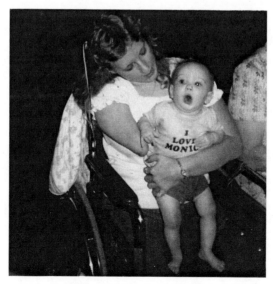

Niece, Nicki, in chair with me.

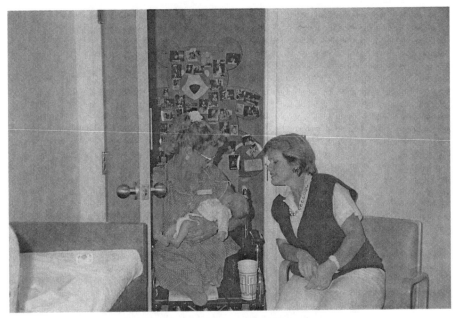
Friend, Jodi with her newborn, Meaghan.

I am so very grateful to each and every parent who allowed me to enjoy their children. I was always very aware of the enormous trust placed in me. There is trust placed in anyone who watches another's children, but there are a few extra details a parent might think about before they leave their kids with me.

I placed enormous pressure on myself. If a child got injured while in my care, I never wanted a parent to wonder if this injury would have happened with a "normal" babysitter. I never wanted to wonder that either. Even usual childhood injuries fell into this category; therefore, I never took any unnecessary risks. I was super careful, super diligent, super attentive, and super focused. I never did anything that I was not absolutely sure I could do when I had kids around. I took no chances. For example, if I was not 100 percent positive I could get a baby out of a baby swing, I did not put them in it. Since I never "practiced" on anyone, I still don't know if I could do this. If I had any uncertainty at all, I did not try.

One day I had an encounter with a parent that shook me hard and remains with me today. I was so profoundly hurt that I was sure I would lose my composure.

I was at the neighborhood park with my neighbors who were celebrating their daughter's five-year-old birthday. There were several kids at the party along with some parents. One of the games was an egg toss, and they needed one more person to help. Not far from me was a woman holding her eight-month-old baby. Her other child was in the egg toss game. I offered to hold him so she could help with the game. All of a sudden, she coiled away from me, started screeching, "No, no no," stood up, and took several steps back, and held her baby very tightly. She had quite obviously disrupted the egg toss, and my neighbor walked toward us. He began to go on about how wonderful I was with kids, but I asked him to stop. I could never hold that baby now—ever.

As I attempted to regroup, I saw a two-year-old black girl toddle over to the same lady (who was still standing and breathing hard) and begin touching the baby's foot. The lady was clearly repulsed again as she raised her baby just above the toddler's reach and discreetly shooed her away with hand gestures. She looked furtively around, hoping that no one saw her but then she saw that I did. I was thoroughly disgusted as I said under my breath, "Well, at least you are an equal opportunity discriminator." I was thankful that the two-year-old simply continued on her merry way, too young to know what just happened to her.

The impact of this one incident was huge and lingered in my heart for a very long time. Suddenly, I was apprehensive about interacting with children. "What if" questions overpowered my common sense. What if I did drop them, what if I can't catch them if they run off, what if I can't pick them up from a fall? Mostly though, I was reminded bitterly that the absolute worst thing about a disability is that people see it before they see you. For this woman and many others, who I was and what I had accomplished with my life did not even register as a possibility.

Everyone has a reaction when they see me. I would have a reaction too if the situation were reversed. It is normal to react. I learned that to some people I would never be anything more than the stereotype they created in their mind, those who sadly would never realize the chasm between their assumptions and reality. The problem for me is that there is no warning as to who they will be or when they will enter my life. It's like being on a constant vigil waiting for the annoying jack-in-the-box to pop up.

My efforts to live normally in an able-bodied world had again suffered a major blow.

CHAPTER 18

UNSOLICITED HELP

Success is not measured by what you accomplish but by the opposition you have encountered and the courage with which you have maintained the struggle against overwhelming odds.
—Orison Swett Marden

SINCE I WAS to go through life with only one limb, I considered myself fortunate to be a congenital amputee rather than traumatic. Because I have never had limbs, I imagine I did not miss them as much as someone who was born with their limbs and then lost them traumatically. I never thought I was different from anyone else unless I was reminded by someone staring or offering unsolicited help.

Reminders of a disability come in a variety of ways. Many people offer assistance out of pity and a misunderstanding or perception that help is needed. Every time someone feels sorry for me, I feel diminished. While it may look like a task is difficult and that help is needed, often it is not difficult but simply a different way to do something.

I know people often struggle with whether or not to offer help when they see a disabled person. Ironically, that very struggle *is* the answer. If you have to wonder, then don't offer. While every situation is different, it is important to note that a disabled person knows very well their limitations. If they cannot do an activity without help, they will have help with them. If they are alone and have not asked for help, then assume they can do what they are doing without help. In addition, most people will ask if they need help.

There have been occasions where people say loudly to me as if I were deaf, "It is so nice that they let you guys out for an afternoon." Out from where? I did hear one woman explain to the store clerk that "homes were doing great things these days." It is sometimes hard to keep my mouth shut. I am frequently amused when someone stands on the mat of an automatic door for me—the kind of door that opens when you step on it. Of course, if they are standing on it, then my wheelchair cannot get past them. Sometimes I am not amused. Sometimes it is just plain tiring.

After a swimming lesson at the YMCA, I changed in the locker room with the rest of the women. Many would stare at me intently with a look of shock or disbelief, not bothered at all that I caught them watching. A few seemed amazed at how I could dress myself, hook my bra, and button a shirt. They would nudge others to watch too. They bragged as if they had contributed in some epic way to my incredible talent. I know these ladies never realized how bad I wanted to disappear.

In a restaurant, it is embarrassing when a presumptuous waitress asks anyone but me what I want to order and then seems genuinely surprised that the person in the chair with one arm can actually speak.

I never say anything to the "locker room" type, the rude type, the savior type, the martyr type, the insensitive type, or the well-intentioned type who offered help that I did not ask for or need. I know they mean well. I try to remember how I look at first blush to others. I try to understand that most people are just trying to be helpful. I make a concerted effort to decline graciously offers to assist, but exercising patience and restraint like this is far more difficult than anything I might have been doing.

CHAPTER 19

PHYSICAL CHALLENGES

It's not the disability that defines you.
It's how you deal with the challenges the disability presents.
We have an obligation to the abilities we DO have, not the disability.
—Jim Abbott

I HAVE THOUGHT a lot about how to describe how I physically do some everyday activities, but surprisingly, this has been difficult. It is like asking someone how they walk or breathe. When you are born with a disability, the way you do things is a part of you and you adapt to it.

Let me start with those things that I have found impossible to do with one hand. Yes, there are some things. In a two-handed world, it is often difficult to lift, carry, or open items with one hand. I have a reacher for things too high or things I drop on the floor. Other activities that are challenging with one hand include the following:

- Push-down-and-twist lids (usually on medication bottles). The worst!
- Getting butter off a pad or out of a tiny container. Second worst!
- Putting gas in the van.
- Cutting meat.
- Putting peanut butter in celery.
- Putting toothpaste on a toothbrush.
- Pouring shampoo on my short arm and then racing quickly to scoop it up in my hand before it runs down the sides.
- Turning on a faucet while holding a glass underneath.
- Lifting hot items from the oven or stove.
- Picking up a full laundry basket, especially containing "little" pieces like socks and underwear.

First, I was quite limited in what I could do in my artificial limbs. My focus was always on keeping my balance and not falling. The artificial legs were like bendable stilts. I had to be extremely alert where and how my crutches touched the ground so they would not slip, especially in rain or snow. It was physically and emotionally exhausting to walk very far. Steps were very grueling, if not impossible. I had great difficulty carrying only my purse, and it was not possible to carry anything else like books, groceries, or children. It was hard to push a grocery cart.

The artificial limbs that I had worn since fourth grade eventually posed a significant hindrance to me living independently. They were of no real help physically and were only marginally effective cosmetically. I sometimes reflected on the prospect of bringing a guy home following a date and then having the awkwardness of stripping off two limbs and scooting around on the floor. I couldn't think of a good way to bring this up in advance either.

I always preferred to be out of the artificial limbs. I could scrub, sweep, dust, change the sheets, or vacuum by scooting on the floor. I was fast too (just like I was during my at bat at Grandma's house). I used arm and my butt, one after the other, creating a walk-like action. I climbed onto furniture to reach higher things. I climbed onto a chair to do dishes or laundry. I never went out in public without my limbs, but I was seen occasionally riding a skateboard down the street to the neighbor's house and once riding a motorcycle with my brother. I still ask myself, "What were you thinking?"

Monica with brother, David, on a motorcycle.

I knew artificial limbs were not the answer if I wanted to live independently. I also knew that going from limbs to a wheelchair would have to be done in California and not Nebraska. Aside from the obvious accessibility issues in Nebraska, there was much family reluctance to a wheelchair. Despite this, I could not live independently with these restrictive limbs, so just like the arm, the legs had to go.

With a new electric wheelchair, I could carry my own groceries, push a grocery cart, run errands, shop, and carry a baby. I could walk beside a young child and hold his or her hand. I could reach higher shelves in the kitchen and closets. I could carry a laundry basket full of clothes. A huge weight had lifted as I no longer had to be mindful of every step I took. The calluses on my body from years of crutches and artificial limbs started to fade. I could slide easily back and forth from my chair to the bed or couch. I could shop in the mall for hours and carry what I bought! I could even eat an ice cream cone or carry a soda while I "walked."

Housework became almost enjoyable. I could sweep, scrub, and vacuum without being constantly on the floor. I could reach the sink to wash dishes. My whole existence was less of a struggle. The biggest advantage to me, however, was the ability to safely carry a baby from one place to the next.

My newly equipped van had hand controls, a wheelchair lift, and two front seats. The driver's seat swiveled backward so I could slide onto it and swiveled forward to drive. My wheelchair locked into place so it could not move around. The freedom I felt was palpable.

There were a few disadvantages. A wheelchair required more physical space than limbs. Public stares increased. For a short time, I tried wearing limbs purely for cosmesis. They were not functional in any way. There were toes on the feet and hose on the legs. The shoe size was six and a half with a one-inch heel. Clerks in the shoe stores looked around to spot the Candid Camera when I asked to see shoes in a size six and a half with a one-inch heel. I was not supposed to stand up in them, but I had to just once.

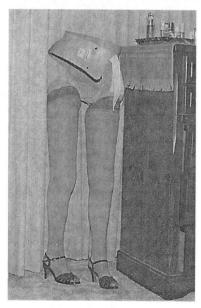

Picture of artificial limbs
for cosmetic use only.

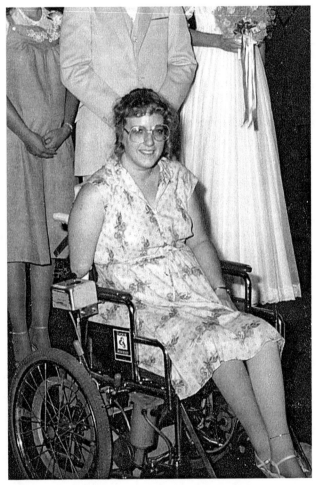

Cosmetic limbs used at my brother's wedding.

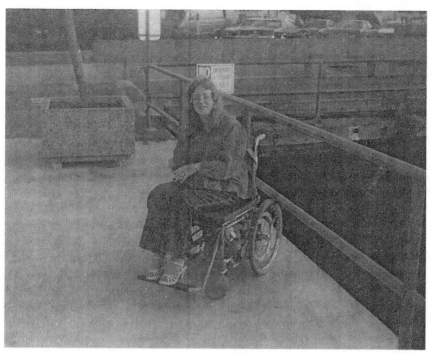

Cosmetic limbs worn on a date with Mike.

Sitting in a chair in my cosmetic limbs.

Standing once in my cosmetic limbs.

Sitting with my legs crossed
in my cosmetic limbs.

Sitting in a chair with my cosmetic limbs.

Cosmetic limbs worn at
my sister's wedding.

CHAPTER 20

EMOTIONAL CHALLENGES

The best years of your life are the ones in which
you decide your problems are your own.
You do not blame them on your mother, the ecology, or the president.
You realize that you control your own destiny.
—Albert Ellis

MANY HAVE ASKED how I moved forward each day coping with such a significant, endless, always-present obstacle, how I managed to go on with seemingly tireless determination and a positive attitude, how I didn't crumble under the pressure. Well, those are good questions. I wonder those things too. I did not feel like a hero though. I didn't feel like I was inspirational. Living with a disability is just a lifestyle—it doesn't make one courageous, brave, or heroic.

It wasn't until I was nearly twenty years old that it hit me that I may be somewhat different. Until then, I had done everything every other girl did—grew up, went to college, chose a career, got a job, anticipated a future. There had not yet been much reason to view my life as negative or depressing or difficult. Although I was clearly aware that there were some things I could never do (like steps), I just had to work around that—either find a way or move on. The steps were not going to change or disappear, and no amount of determination or spunk of mine would change them into a ramp.

Before I was twenty, I don't recall giving much thought to barriers. My parents very quietly worked around the obvious. A good example is my dad building the porch on the farmhouse and my bedroom out of a pantry. Mom would always cut my meat, peel my oranges, and cut triangles in the grapefruit halves so the bites would easily spoon out. We made quite the duo with her holding open a glove and me sliding all five fingers into the five slots.

I was expected to do chores just as the other kids were expected to do:

for example, dishes, making my bed, laundry, cleaning bathrooms, husking corn, and ironing to name a few. My parents always made sure I had a different chore to do in exchange for one I could not do. For example, if the other kids were in the garden picking cucumbers, my job was to wash them. Goodness, just how many cucumbers did I wash? And as long as I am asking, how many shirts did I iron? Was that even legal?! If the other kids were in the pasture cutting thistles, I was cleaning the kitchen and/or baking a cake. If the other kids were carrying buckets of water to the new trees my dad planted (probably 100!), I was sitting at the well pumping the buckets full of water. Incidentally, these trees grew into a significant windbreak, shielding that farm home from the north wind. It looks so much different than the little saplings with a ring of water around them.

So now to the question: how did I do it? First, I had to make big things small in order to get through each day. All my energy and focus had to be on the truly important things like accessibility of a bathroom. I could not spend much mental or physical time on things that really did not matter or that I could not change. I was expert at finding alternatives.

I had to make concessions and know when to make them. I had to perfect the art of compromise. I had to be content to watch from the sidelines and even perhaps credit someone else for an idea I slipped them. I had to be very patient and extremely tolerant. I had to take perseverance to a new level. I had to be creative and organized. I had to learn quickly how to anticipate barriers, how to think and plan ahead, and how to make sudden new plans for "what to do if."

Most importantly perhaps, I realized there was no choice. Life went on. I realized quickly that if I lamented too long over things I couldn't do, then I could be quickly consumed with negative thoughts. I had to mentally concentrate on the things I could do. When I did that, I was always grateful. For the most part, I coped well. It often took other people or events to remind me that I was disabled. It always hurt the most when I didn't see it coming, like losing a job promotion, someone freaking when I offered to hold their baby, or when I wanted to travel somewhere.

Inherently, I knew that my attitude would be the key to accessing and retaining the help I would need. I had to be very adaptable. I had to give much thought to the biorhythm and timing of others. I could not be demanding, rude, or disrespectful. I could not burn any bridges. I understood clearly that I would never be completely free or completely in control.

I would be fully dependent on artificial limbs, wheelchairs, van lifts, and hand controls. If any one of those things needed repair, I was stuck. There was usually little to no warning before my chair would just stop or my lift would not go up or down. If I was in the van, I could not get out. If I was out of the van, I could not get in. I could be stopped in my tracks without warning. Many times, a breakdown would happen on a Friday night or a three-day weekend where help was either unavailable or very expensive. The countless possibilities were always in the back of my mind. I became the master planner of "what if."

Disabled parking was another challenge. These spots are typically closer to the entrance and much wider than usual, which makes it very convenient to get a wheelchair in between to load groceries. In addition, a side lift is not possible in a regular parking spot. I always had a back lift because finding a usable disabled parking space is very challenging.

The most common users of disabled parking, however, almost never have an obvious disability. In addition, they usually run into the store. They drive amazing sports cars and monster trucks.

If they see me, then I hear a litany of unbidden explanations. "Oh, I'm sorry, I just went in for a minute, my 'family member' is disabled (not present), I had surgery a while back, I usually never do but . . . " I must admit, it gives me pleasure to watch them squirm. I don't have to do or say anything—I just smile. The same thing happens with the bathroom stalls.

Life as a triple amputee has been very challenging, exhausting, and yes, even depressing. It is not easy to maintain a positive outlook amid unbridled injustices. Some days the struggle is great and I worry it will overtake me. The good-intentioned expectations of others are often a doubled-edged sword.

Consider the usual and customary preparations necessary prior to taking a trip—what to pack, how much to pack, cleaning up loose ends at work, perhaps training a substitute, hotel reservations, accessories for camping, how much cash is needed, plane reservations, rent-a-car, packing, who will care for pets, who will get the mail, who will get the newspaper—the the list goes on. Now consider in addition to all that, accessibility of all bathrooms, homes, hotels, campgrounds, airplanes, self-serve gas stations, cars, and similar concerns.

A great example of "best laid plans" is a trip Mike and I took to the Grand Canyon for our 20th wedding anniversary in 2009. I made the hotel arrangements and confirmed weekly. I confirmed the reservations on the day before we left. The drive was about 5 hours. We were very excited.

Once the van is packed with suitcases, a shower chair, my wheelchair, and other assistive devices, I cannot get out until Mike unloads. We eat in the car and we don't stop to visit places along the way. If needed, I pee in a plastic bottle. I am quite adept at not needing a restroom—a skill I learned in grade school. Still I must ration what I drink and how much.

When we arrived at the hotel, Mike went to check in. Incredibly, he was told that our room had been rented to someone else. They were very apologetic and offered us their biggest suite. Mike looked at the suite. It was wonderful but the bathroom was not accessible. He came back to the car where I was waiting. I was anxious to unpack and see the sights. He said our room was not available and they had no other room. What? At first, I did not believe him—I had been so careful to confirm our reservation. He got in the car and stated that there was no room—we would have to find a different hotel.

We spent the next couple of hours checking the other hotels. None of them had a disabled room.

While Mike and I were discussing our options, including going back home, the hotel with our original reservation called and said our room was now available. Apparently, they had asked the occupants to move to the available suite. The whole ordeal took about 3 hours. Events like this are a part of our travel reality.

Accessibility to everything everywhere is a luxury I can only dream about. I am often envious of trips all over the world taken by others and how there is no thought given to barriers at all. That is because there won't be any barriers for them. It is such a foreign thought. I am limited in what I can do and where I can go. For example, a bathroom may be accessible, but I need the toilet handrail on the right side. If it is on the left, the toilet is virtually impossible for me to use. Many showers are roll-in showers, but I cannot take my electric chair in them. The list of things I silently deal with goes on. I must anticipate all the barriers I will face and whether or not I can find a solution for all of them. If even one barrier remains, the entire trip may not be possible. Put simply—a curb might as well be a flight of stairs. I must always think ahead, ask for details, and be prepared.

When I decline to attend a social event or activity, it is usually not because I don't want to go. In fact, it is usually the complete opposite. I am struggling inside because I want to go, but an event may have more barriers than are feasible to overcome. The older I get, the more burdensome the barriers become; for example, I can no longer jump from my chair to the floor in order to scoot into a bathroom. Most importantly, however, protecting my only arm must always be the determining factor in any decision I make. Grandma knew then what I so acutely know now.

I choose not to speak of this inner struggle because it is, quite simply, mine to carry. Not sharing, however, does not mean all is rosy. Discussion of this topic with others typically makes them uncomfortable and helpless and solves nothing. My life is much, much easier to maneuver through if there is no pity. I fought relentlessly to maintain a "normal" life, thinking this would keep pity at bay. However, I now understand that this may be a rational reaction to a triple amputee and will likely always exist. On those occasions when I am forced to make difficult decisions, I ask that people stop to realize just how much they don't understand about what it takes for me to maneuver through each day, no matter how easy I make it look.

CHAPTER 21

PRECONCEIVED IDEAS AND STEREOTYPES

Other people's opinion of you does not have to become your reality.
—Les Brown

PEOPLE WHO SEE me for the first time typically have very stereotypical thoughts. As noted, I have come to realize that this is logical; however, one of the biggest frustrations in my life is the huge gap between what people assume about me and the person I really am. It is often hard for me to figure out where I fit—in the able-bodied world or in the disabled world.

This disparity has always irritated me. Tearing down the flawed first impressions and erroneous preconceived ideas is tedious and very tiring. For many years, I believed that if I was persistent, one day the walls would fall. As I matured, however, I realized I would never change that first impression and that it would be present initially with every new person I met.

Some of the totally inaccurate assumptions attributed to me include not working, not driving, being mentally challenged, and needing assisted living, personal care, housekeeping, and nursing. Many quickly assumed that I was not only mentally challenged but also on multiple federal and state aid programs, welfare, food stamps, and disability. It is usually presumed that I am the patient when I accompany someone to the doctor or when I picked up my transcription work from an office.

One such mistaken assumption presented itself on my wedding day in a comical way. The wedding and reception were over and the guests were dispersing throughout the casino to play slots or cards or something. My sister wanted to pull some slots, so I was holding her five-month-old daughter, Lindsey. Soon a security guard descended on me and said that the baby could not be in the casino even though she was asleep. So I took her out of the gaming area to a quiet place by the door where I watched people and Lindsey continued to sleep.

After about twenty minutes, someone scurried by quickly and threw something in my water cup that was attached to my chair. I was startled by the splashing water, but before I could react, a second person also tossed something into my cup. Both people had thrown coins! Just as I was realizing this, a third person threw in a dollar bill. None of them stopped—they just kept walking. Okay, I get it now. They thought I was panhandling. I guess I looked in need of assistance—such a pitiful sight with a baby and all. Now I had dirty coins and paper money floating in my water. These reactions were always so different from the reality of my true life.

Incidentally, the amount thrown into my cup that night was exactly $1.42. Looks like I would have had to sit there for a long while if I wanted to buy formula or diapers!

One of the more hurtful, wrong, and unfair assumptions is that my husband is my nursemaid. While Mike does a lot of things for me as my spouse, I also do a lot of things for him as his spouse. He readily admits that he got the better end of that deal. The list of things Mike does for me *solely* because of my disability is relatively short. When I asked him, he answered, "Well, really nothing. I change the calendars, I change the bedding, I put gas in the van (self-serve gas stations have totally precluded me from getting gas by myself any longer). There really isn't anything else that I can think of."

I thought of a few more—he puts my hair in a ponytail, he closes a necklace or bracelet, he cuts my meat, he cuts watermelons in half, and he puts soda in the fridge. Other chores are simply in the category of a helpful and considerate spouse, much like he expects from me, much like a "normal" couple.

Mike has never once painted my fingernails or helped me dress. He has never helped me bathe. He did help me once with personal hygiene for two days following carpal tunnel surgery on my *only* hand. No detail necessary. Both of us were very anxious about the obvious implications of a bad outcome. Not only was he extremely supportive and reassuring, but he also turned out to be the best nurse. He truly understood both the physical and emotional aspects.

There is no question that Mike has made my life infinitely easier. He customized my first home office so that for the first time my desk was the correct height for me. He put holes in the table for plug strips so I didn't have to reach under-the-table outlets. He put on/off switches within reach so when a service person said "unplug the modem and plug it back in," I could reach it. He made various keyboard risers at varying heights. He made an adjustable tripod for my transcription foot pedal. Genius! That was indeed a true work of art. Another work of art is the lazy Susan–type bookcase he made for my medical reference books. I only need to spin this around to reach my thirty-plus books.

Lazy-Susan-type bookcase designed and built by Mike.

Another view of the lazy-Susan-type bookcase.

Mike can fix anything around the house and also my chair, van, and wheelchair lift. After I met him, my "stranded time" due to malfunctioning equipment decreased remarkably. He has designed and built countless ramps. He added an extender on the handle of my razor and one on my deodorant bottle so I could more easily reach under my left arm with my left hand.

There are no preconceived ideas or preformed notions when I first meet a child. My chair is usually a curiosity, a cool toy, something to climb. Ramps are great for tricycles and skateboards. I am thankful for each and every kid in my life. I now know that each one of them, individually and collectively, helped me navigate through this disability. They saw me as I saw myself.

CHAPTER 22

DISCRIMINATION AND UNFAIRNESS

*Sometimes the strongest people are the ones
who love beyond all faults,
cry behind closed doors,
and fight battles that nobody knows about.*
—Unknown

DESPITE MY EARLY naiveté, I was aware that I was physically different. I just had no reason to believe it mattered. I genuinely believed that discrimination did not exist. As I got older, I was ill prepared to handle the discrimination, bias, and unfairness I would face. After all, I really had my hands full handling misguided first impressions. I had to grow quickly a "thick skin" as I came face-to-face with all types of unfairness and, yes, even prejudice.

Discrimination in the workplace still happens today, but it is easily camouflaged with plausible reasons like "someone else is better qualified." I have no sound explanation for the many jobs I applied for but did not get. I was wiser than I was with my first job when I was told that "future applicants might feel uncomfortable," but there were several times when I believed again that my physical appearance was the reason. Eventually I did not apply for jobs that were "out in the open," but this made little difference either. Finally, I liked it when transcription jobs could be done at home. I made a careful, calculated effort *not* to reveal my disability to anyone because it had no effect on my job performance in any way. Wow! What a totally different world it is without a disability. Eventually I told my closest coworkers, but not until my job performance preceded it.

I have some illustrations of unfairness. It is difficult to "see" every disability, but some, like mine, are quite obvious, and there are not many advantages or benefits that come with it. Going to an amusement park is a perfect example of ridiculous. I must pay the exact same amount as those who can ride everything, do everything, and stand up to see everything even though I will clearly not have access to everything. To me, this lacks common sense.

Another even more ludicrous example happened when I took my MT certification exam at a test center. Everyone was almost strip-searched to make sure nothing was taken into the exam room. When I registered for the exam weeks earlier, I had to "declare" any special needs, and I told them of my one-inch flat board that I placed under the keyboard for added height. I was told this was fine. However, when I got to the testing site, no such permission could be found, and they would not allow me to take this keyboard riser into the testing room. I could not believe it, and for the first time in a long time, I didn't know what to do.

Already stressed and edgy about taking such an important test, now I also felt sick. It took everything I had inside not to break down. To me, this was insane. How could my physical appearance limit my opportunities but count for nothing when I had a need that was so plainly obvious?

I wanted to hide as multiple attempts were made to contact the permissions department. Others were now arriving for their tests, and I was embarrassed. I was so very upset. This was not fairness. I was not asking for any special advantage. Finally, permission was granted on the phone, but by this time the damage had been done. It was hard to refocus on the test. I could barely keep from crying, and I wanted to run out the door. While I did pass the test and become a CMT (certified medical transcriptionist), this type of needless barrier made my life more difficult. Once again, I was reminded of my disability, a fact I did not think about too often.

Next is an example of unreasonable. After dealing with carpal tunnel symptoms for quite some time, finally in 2007, I realized that I needed surgery. I had a great hand surgeon in San Diego who had performed an uneventful trigger-thumb release, but we now lived in Pahrump. I carefully and purposefully researched until I found someone I considered skilled. I was very afraid of carpal tunnel surgery. Results were often mixed, and I only had *one* hand.

Mike and I went to the appointment. First we were made to wait almost three hours before being seen. When the doctor finally arrived, he stopped abruptly in the door as if he saw a ghost. It took him a minute to gain his composure enough to even speak. He was wearing no less than four pairs of gloves, yet he put on another in our presence. He never touched me. He read my chart on the computer, said I definitely needed surgery, but then began listing many reasons why he couldn't do this. One reason was that he operated in a surgicenter and not a hospital. What? Why did that matter? He suggested that I see his partner who did operate in a hospital. I had already decided that I did not trust this germophobe with my only hand. He was clearly afraid of a lawsuit. Our appointment lasted four minutes after which we spent twenty-five minutes in line to pay for our visit.

The next week we saw his partner. The visit went a bit better, but I did not like this doctor either. Just like the first doctor, I certainly did not feel confident in giving him my only hand.

Finally, Worker's Compensation scheduled me with a doctor who specialized in treating carpal tunnel surgery failures, cases where the first surgery did not go well. When this doctor walked into the room, he exuded confidence. He saw the challenge before him but unequivocally stated he could fix it. I definitely could relinquish my hand to him. However, there was one other issue—he stated that Worker's Compensation, after discussion with my employer, felt that my carpal tunnel was likely due more to my "life circumstances" than it was to typing for all my adult life. Really? It sounded to me that Worker's Comp was trying to bail out from paying for it.

My last nerve had just been stomped upon. This poor doctor got the brunt of my frustration. I told him that this was unacceptable, and I considered it reverse discrimination or unfairness. Was he really saying that I could never have a legitimate work-related carpal tunnel claim even though I typed for my entire career? And what life circumstances count here? I didn't do anything unusual with my hand—I used it normally doing normal things just like anyone else, so why would I not be eligible for treatment of the most common hand injury caused by typing?

He said he understood my point, and I heard nothing more about this. My surgery was very successful. No more numbness or tingling. I had no pain from the surgery itself and needed no pain pills. However, because I had to use my hand for every transfer to the bed, toilet, bathtub, car, etc., I had pain for six months. I sometimes wonder though, had I not stood my ground, if my "life circumstances" would have canceled a Worker's Comp claim.

Other frustrations include not being able to buy long-term disability insurance, fly on a plane without being catheterized (by whom on each end is never divulged), ride in or drive any other vehicle, or buy clothing. Long-sleeved clothes need to be rolled up, which creates lots of unpleasant bulk.

I often envisioned a home that was 100 percent customized for my disability, a place where I did not have to accommodate a thing. I saw several such homes on the *Home Makeover* show, and I was often jealous. No matter how hard I try, I can't envision a life without barriers or what it would be like to get on a plane, travel in any size car, not wait for a lift to rise or lower, stay at a friend's home, step over toys on the floor, or travel anywhere in the world. Most of all though, I wonder what it would be like to never again wonder about bathroom accessibility.

I wonder what it is like to walk barefoot on grass, sand, or smooshy carpet, to wear high heels and hose, to hold an infant and feed him at the same time, to run, to walk in the rain, or to go up or downstairs or bleachers. I wonder what it is like to do two things at once using both hands.

I never believed it was society's responsibility to make sure I could do everything I wanted to do. Having no ramp or elevator available was a major problem for me, but I never thought someone else should provide them. If a building or someone's home was not accessible, I did not go in. Admittedly, it was not an ideal situation, but I had accepted it as a fact of my life. After all, accessibility in California was significantly better than it was in Nebraska, and I was sure I had found heaven on earth.

On July 26, 1990, Pres. George H. Bush Sr. signed into law the Americans with Disabilities Act. This made it mandatory for any public building, new or old, to provide wheelchair accessibility for the entrance and bathroom. New construction had to meet new standards. A deadline was also put in place to retrofit most every public building, no matter how old. This had a huge impact on accessibility in the United States and was great for me. Instead of avoiding inaccessible places, soon I could go almost anywhere without much difficulty. It was a huge step forward.

When you meet someone with a disability, I know it can be awkward. Many people have told me that they just don't know what to say or do. Here are a few hints what *not* to say or do.

"You don't have it so bad—you'd better never complain." I often hear this from someone after they see a disability that they perceive is worse than mine. I wonder, How do you know what rank to give my disability versus the other? How can you even presume what it is like every minute of every day? For these people, I wish they would spend twenty-four hours in a wheelchair with their feet never touching the floor. They would see quickly the many barriers and perhaps realize how much they take for granted.

"You have been so lucky." It took me a while to digest this one. Lucky. How

do you figure? Beyond being simply unbelievable, it negates all of my effort in making a successful life with this disability.

"Oh, that happens to everybody." I get this response when I mention an ailment of an ordinary kind, like arthritis. Indeed, it might happen to everybody, but not too many are starting at the place I am. I have an extra layer on which any "normal" ailment will start. The consequences are also larger—I have no body part to spare.

"Just cut off my legs." I heard a woman state that if her cosmetically treated varicose veins did not start to look better soon, she would rather just have her legs cut off. I am doubtful that this was even said in jest. As the last word came out of her mouth, she saw me. She had nowhere to hide. She knew I had heard her. While it was certainly an awkward moment for me, I doubt seriously that it influenced her in the slightest.

Don't pat a person in a wheelchair on the head. That is so condescending.

Don't lean on a wheelchair or rest your foot on it. Consider a wheelchair part of someone's personal space.

Don't assume that a disabled person is the patient in a medical office. He or she may just be accompanying a friend or family member.

Don't feel bad if you use a common word like *walk* or *run*. This is not offensive to a wheelchair user, and in fact, is often not even noticed.

It is uncomfortable and awkward to carry on a conversation looking up at someone. It is much easier if both are sitting at the same level. This is especially important for longer conversations.

Don't park in disabled parking spaces—not even for a "minute." They exist for a reason.

I understand it is difficult to determine when to ask a disabled person if they need help. My best advice is to let them ask you. For example, I can grocery shop by myself. However, if an item is out of my reach or too heavy, I will ask for assistance. No one has ever refused to help me. Keep in mind that just because something looks difficult or awkward to you, it does not mean that it is difficult or awkward for the person you want to help. Most disabled people will ask if they need help.

CHAPTER 23

FROM MY SIBLINGS' POINT OF VIEW

Being happy doesn't mean everything is perfect.
It means you've decided to look beyond the imperfections.
—Unknown

I AM THE oldest of seven kids. I have four brothers and two sisters. I often wondered what it was like for them growing up with my disability. Just like me, they were not given any special training, education, or even discussion about the obvious disabilities I had. It just went without saying that nothing was really different, and yet some things were quite different, especially for them. No one really ever complained too loudly. Mom had a favorite saying, which she still uses today: "It's a long way from the heart." Of all the things she had to deal with, some things were quite simply very petty. However, there were times when we all had issues that did not seem petty to us. Looking back, all of us would have benefited from some meaningful conversations and discussions of these things.

Much, much later, I learned the truth of the "thistle story." This story lives on today when we need a laugh. It has survived the test of time and provides much insight into our family dynamic.

While we lived on the acreage, everyone had chores. One of these chores was cutting thistles from our pasture. A thistle is a prickly plant with a flowery head containing seeds, which are spread with the wind. If the flowery head is not removed, thistles will overtake a pasture or a field growing a crop. Since the flowery head is pinkish purple, thistles are quite visible, which causes anxiety for neighbors too.

I was not required to go out into the pasture to cut thistles, but I had different chores in the house to do when the other kids were out there. Dad arranged with the kids that they would each get one penny for every thistle they cut, but they would be required to split their total amount with me. I had no idea until later just how unfair this "policy" seemed to them. Of course, it would be confusing. Somehow, without much discussion, we all had to figure out that on the one hand I was not different really, but yet sometimes I *was* different. This distinction was not always obvious, and certainly it was not obvious to young kids.

One night, I was babysitting and all of us had gone to bed. About an hour later, my brother, then about age seven, came to my room very upset, but he said he could not tell me why. He got in bed with me and we chatted for a bit, but he still would not tell me why he was so upset. He kept saying, "I can't tell you because it is so bad." I was definitely getting worried at the secret he was holding. Finally, when it seemed like he was almost asleep, he just blurted out, "Did you know that you can never eat a Whopper?" I asked why and he explained, "Because it takes two hands to handle the Whopper." It was all I could do not to laugh, but I didn't because he was truly so upset over that fact. I reassured him that I would most certainly be able to eat a Whopper. He seemed relieved and went back upstairs to bed. Interesting things on the minds of my siblings! Who knew! This same brother calls me his half-sister. Every family needs a comedian.

One summer night at our local county fair, a concession worker asked my sister what happened to me. My sister, then about age nine, answered, "She was in a bad accident." As she walked away, she immediately regretted her answer. She knew I had not been in an accident at all, but it was at that moment that she first realized she did not know the answer to that question.

The following are excerpts from my brothers and sisters. I think their thoughts are best told in their own words. I have not attributed the names to each comment because it does not matter who said what. I learned a lot from their comments and I am grateful for their honesty. In addition, I asked Mom a series of "What was it like?" questions, and her comments are at the end.

****

I remember the very first time I knew she was in our family. We were in Lincoln, and it was in front of Sacred Heart School. Monica was there for grades two, three, four, five, and part of six. There is a picture of her with the family in her First Communion dress. I wasn't even in first grade yet. I might have been four. I remember going to this Sacred Heart School one time with Mom to pick Monica up. Finally it dawned on me that she was coming home with us. I was mortified. This is the earliest time I can remember that it finally registered with me that she was my sister. It's my first memory of her.

**

I was always her savior. Every time she saw a bug, she knew she could rely on me to come kill it. She was petrified of them. Everybody else would say they caught it and killed it, but most times they did not. If they didn't, then the bug would be back in a few minutes. She got to where she wanted to see the dead bug. I always killed them. I emptied out her entire closet once looking for a cricket. I found him.

**

For Halloween, she would dress up and we would pull her along in a little red wagon for trick-or-treating. She would sit in the street many times while we went to the door and got candy. We always had her bag with us if the wagon could not get to the door. If the weather was bad and she could not go with us, we all had to pour our candy in the middle of the floor and split it evenly and share with Monica. We always had to add Monica in.

**

When I was in elementary school, Monica was in the seventh grade, which was upstairs. Because of these steps, she did not go to lunch or recess. I was responsible to get Monica's lunch to her. I would go to lunch, go play for about ten minutes, run back to the basement cafeteria, get her lunch, and run it up to the third floor. Then I would run out the door to try to catch my place at bat. It never occurred to me to eat with her.

**

Monica always had to do her share of the housework. She would climb up on a chair and wash the dishes.

**

When I was a freshman at the University of Nebraska, Monica was a senior. There were times when she needed help getting to class in the snow. I would have to put my foot on each side of the crutch so she could take a step. At that time of my life, I hated doing that, and I voiced that to her. I remember one time I did not help her to class and I don't know if she had to skip class or what. I have felt guilty about that ever since. I don't know how she got home from class.

****

I remember when she got that orange Chevy Nova. It was the envy of my life. She worked at Lincoln General, and I would take her there on winter days and then I would get to drive it home. It was so awesome! Then I had to go get her and occasionally she would say, "I would like to drive home." I remember a lot of resentment having to do all that stuff. I was into myself and whatever freshmen were into. She was a senior when I was a freshman. I remember a time around Thanksgiving we went to somebody's apartment and stayed there instead of going home to Norfolk because the weather was too bad. I walked to Valentino's in the cold. There was snow up to my knees. I walked home and we had pizza. I would give anything for those four days back.

****

I remember one time when Monica was home in the summer right after graduation. I was still in high school. It was summertime, and I got a part-time job that I could walk to. I washed dishes at a restaurant. It was just a little back-room station where you ran the dishes through a steamer and pulled them back out. Monica wanted so badly to have a job and make some money, so she said, "Do you think there is anything I could do there?" We decided to try but agreed that we would not say that I was her sister. She went in and filled out an application. The owner came back and told me that this handicapped girl came in to apply for a job. Not knowing "this handicapped girl" was my sister, she went on to say, "I don't know what she thought she could do for us!"

****

All of us remember her "reserve." That is what we called her short arm. Instead of hitting us, she would put the reserve on our thigh and push down. It really hurt. She was strong and could usually pin us down after she caught us. I am still afraid of that reserve. We all are.

****

We used to go to church in Syracuse every Sunday and would take up a whole pew. Monica would get up and go to Communion on her legs. Invariably, by the time she stood up and slid sideways out of the pew, she would always be the last one in line. Everyone would be done with Communion and be waiting for her to go all the way around the entire stack of pews. Dad would have to get up and out of his seat to let her back in. It was to the point where every time we had Communion, I would think, "Oh, here we go!" That got embarrassing to me. We were always making a scene at Communion. It was just a constant reminder that we were different. Our family was different.

****

When we lived on the acreage, we rode the school bus to school. Every day, Mother would have to meet the school bus and drag Monica on or off the bus. Mom would step onto the first step. Monica would put her back to the door. Mom would grab her under her arms and drag her up one step at a time. I was mortified. They dropped us younger kids off at school first so I don't know who got Monica off the bus once she got to school. This was how she got on and off the bus even in high school. Of course, all of us kids are already seated on the bus, again waiting for Mom and Monica.

****

In the summer of 1971, when Monica had surgery at orthopedic hospital, I remember we had to pile in the car and go see her on the weekends. I hated that. We'd get to the hospital and say, "Hi, Monica," and then we would be bored stiff. We would get there as early as we could and stay until visiting hours were over. I would say that Mom and Dad didn't spend extra attention on Monica. They only spent what her needs required. Sometimes, like for hospital stays, her needs required a little more time from them.

****

I told Monica once that I thought she was lucky. It just seemed that everything went great for her. She really took issue with my choice of words— lucky. She said she would change places with me for even just one day. Would I be willing to do the same? I wasn't.

****

Dad was a fair man. He insisted that Monica be treated fairly. If we were outside working, she was inside scrubbing floors. I will have the image of her scrubbing floors forever. She was never able to use her physical condition as an excuse ever.

****

She had to do everything we all had to do. She got no special accommodations. I never gave it much thought that she was different.

****

She never missed *Hawaii Five-O*. She would dance around in the middle of the living room floor like crazy to the music. If you made even a sound when the show was on, she would literally chase you into a corner and grind her little arm into our thigh or our shoulder. You could never outrun Monica. She would get you in the corner of a bedroom or the living room and you were toast!

****

Mom and Dad's time was not taken up with Monica. She did not really get any special treatment.

****

Monica is the only one I know who can make her bed without getting out of it.

****

People always stared. I'm sure there were times when I thought, "Take a picture, it will last longer," but we were just so used to her that I guess even if they did have a reaction, we did not make a big deal about it, mainly because Monica didn't. She knew she was different, and we never knew her any other way. She was different from us, but I don't think I ever got wigged out when somebody looked at her funny. It was the only way I ever knew her.

****

The fact that she is married. I mean, how did she meet a guy? How did she date a guy? How did she manage that? I mean, think about it. That's a marvel. Who allows themselves to fall in love with that prospect?

I don't mean to say that I'm such a martyr because I do a few things for her. But people like Monica can only do so few things so you want to do them for her. So in a weird way, it affects my life. It is not a complaint, it is a reality.

Mom's Comments

What was it like with so many kids?

I never thought about it. I never thought I had too many kids. I actually thought I might be "bringing the average down" because one of my brothers had twelve kids and another brother had ten. I never once thought my kids were too much trouble. Life was never boring. I was very organized; you had to be organized with seven kids. I could turn a penny into a nickel most of the time. I don't remember a typical morning getting ready for school, but you kids were all ready for the school bus with your paper lunch sack in hand when it came.

It was just my job. I didn't know any other way of life.

I spent a lot of time cooking. I always had a snack ready after school.

I always had supper on the table. Every Sunday I stood at the stove for two hours making crepe pancakes one at a time. Sometimes we got Tastee Treat hamburgers because they were only ten cents on Tuesdays.

I have never had a kid with a broken bone, out of all my kids.

I never missed a home game when any of my kids were playing ball.

What was it like grocery shopping? Did you take kids with you?

I suppose I did once in a while, but really I don't remember ever having kids with me while I shopped for groceries or otherwise.

What did you and Dad do for entertainment?

We went out to eat almost every Friday night. We got a sitter for you kids until you, Monica, were old enough to do it. We both loved to dance and we did that a lot. We were good dancers.

When you babysat, what did all of us play?

You liked to play school with the kids. We also had a big fenced-in backyard with a nice swing set and a huge tractor tire full of sand. Many times I set up the hose so you could run through the sprinkler.

Did you sit outside while we played?

No, I checked on you from the window. I made sure everyone was accounted for and upright, and then I continued with my chores.

How long did it take to do laundry for such a crowd?

I did the laundry when I needed to, not every day. I always hung the clothes on a clothesline; I didn't use the dryer. I had an electric two-tone green double-tub washer with a wringer. I did a lot of laundry when everyone was sleeping, but I could trust you kids long enough to hang a load on the line. When you kids were younger, I put you in a crib or the playpen when I went outside to hang clothes.

Did Dad help with the kids?

Not usually. It was his job to support us, and he worked days and nights a lot. He sold insurance and had to see farmers at night. Taking care of the kids and the household was my job, but Al had high expectations of the way things should be done. For the most part, he did not babysit, shop, clean, cook, or do laundry. He remodeled every house we lived in (orange was his favorite color). We also had many rental apartments so when a renter moved out, we had to paint the entire apartment. Monica, Dad would lift you into the top cupboards because you fit well and did a fine job painting "hard-to-reach" places. Dad also bought a big Christmas tree every year. He would bring it in the house and set it on the stand, but he did not help decorate it. That was my job.

Dad and I were both exhausted at the end of the day. Sometimes we would watch news together, but I fell asleep every time I sat down so I usually just went straight to bed.

CHAPTER 24

OBSERVATIONS FROM FRIENDS AND FAMILY

The soul is healed by being with children.
—Fyodor Dostoevsky

WRITING THIS BOOK gave me the opportunity to learn a lot about my life when I was too young to remember. The following are excerpts from interviews conducted by Pat with my friends and family. Again, I have attributed no names. It was important for me to truly understand what my disability was like from their perspective. I am very thankful for the cooperation. I am humbled by the comments.

Put all together, I couldn't help but notice the commonalities in the excerpts below. I wonder if one is born with the coping mechanisms necessary to live a disabled life, if they are the result of your upbringing, or a little of both. I suspect a little of both.

****

I know it wasn't easy, but Alvin was a very, very, determined father and he insisted that Monica be raised like the other kids. There was to be no partiality or babying. I remember her scooting down the stairs on her little butt, and in those days, every stairway had two railings so she would go down on the side where she could hold on to with her good arm. You could see how determined she was, but she got it all from her father, Alvin. I know he insisted that Agnes listen to him and not baby her.

****

I never talked to Agnes at all about her birth. I think that was it, because of Monica's deformities that no one said anything. I didn't know how to talk to Agnes. I think Agnes talked to her mom, and I think Alvin talked to his mother. They never said anything to the rest of the family.

****

I don't know what Agnes and Alvin's first thoughts were when they saw the baby because I wasn't there right away. But I never heard them complain. They just took the baby home, and she was normal in every other way.

****

I went along with my parents to Kansas to visit my sister who had given birth to a baby with three missing limbs. At first, my parents initially said I couldn't go because seeing a baby with such severe deformities might cause me not to want kids. I wanted to go, however, and they eventually said okay.

The trip to Kansas was a very quiet one. No one said much, at least not about the new baby. I tried to imagine what a baby with three missing limbs would look like. I didn't know what to expect. When we got to Kansas, Alvin and Agnes took us to the hospital. We went into the room one by one. Soon it was my turn. Slowly, I opened the door and went in.

When I first saw Monica, she was wearing only a diaper and lying on a hospital bed in a room by herself. I was overcome with relief. She did not look as bad as I had imagined. In fact, I thought she was very cute. She was very tiny.

****

My memories of Monica are awesome. I have admired her since the day I first saw her as a four-year-old child and all she went through and the choices she had to make about having the foot taken off and wearing the leg braces. She was always happy and so easy to talk to.

****

She had two real obstacles in life. One was ice and snow and the other was steps, and she could get rid of one by going to California.

****

Alvin and Agnes raised Monica just like they did all the children. They just allowed her to do and be everything that she could do and try to be a part of everything and included in everything. She did chores like sweeping. She just did everything the other kids did.

****

What I remember most about Monica was just that nothing stopped her. She just never let anything be an obstacle. She was an inspiration in that way. No matter what it was, she figured out a solution and did it.

****

When I met Monica, she was four or five. She was really a bright girl, and she was very vocal. She just got along so well with her handicap. Her speech and thinking wasn't affected at all. She always seemed to get along with all the kids. I'm not surprised at all that she is where she is because she did so well. She never said anything; it did not seem to bother her that others were "normal." She just took life head-on and just went through it. She never asked why me or anything.

****

Even at a young age, if people made her mad, Monica would call them a piss ant. I would snicker a bit when I heard this. She didn't have any problem holding her own. She was an outgoing little girl.

****

That's another thing I admire about Monica. She can laugh about her situation and not be bitter and grumpy.

****

She did not let her handicap deter her from doing anything. She would play with all the kids. She'd pick up that bat and hit that ball, and she would run to first base before they could put her out.

****

She could type faster with one hand than most can with two. She could drive a car. She just handled that handicap superbly. She makes a very, very good role model with only one arm. She could sew with a sewing machine. She could embroider and cross-stitch.

The reason she is my hero is because she is so pleasant. She is always giving somebody the benefit of the doubt. She is so empathetic. She has never said poor me, poor me. Her fuse never seems to waiver.

Kids who meet Monica for the first time might ask, "What's wrong with you? Where are your legs?" But usually within fifteen minutes, a kid has warmed up to her and is her best friend. She is soooo good with kids, always has been and always will be.

I remember that Monica was really happy and chipper. She was usually laughing and grinning and playing with the kids.

I would have to say that from what I saw, her parents treated her no differently than any of the other kids.

I never saw her parents treat her differently than any of the other kids. She didn't get special attention. They didn't make concessions for her. It wasn't something that you ever mentioned.

My kids are the lucky ones for having Monica in their lives.

Our kids look at disabilities differently because of their exposure to Monica and her positive attitude.

Many people babysit kids, but Monica truly loved kids, each one, all of them. And the kids loved her within minutes. I noticed this with all kids—she always had kids around her. They got protective of her, some of them. It was cute.

****

I don't know how I would have done it without her help. She was patient and kind with my kids, and she could always comfort them.

****

The proof is in how much kids like her. I never saw a child who did not like her, even those at school where their only contact was maybe fifteen minutes.

****

My kids talked constantly about her.

****

My kids did not clap by using hand to hand. They always clapped hand to elbow, the way they saw Monica do it.

****

Monica was in my life when I was a young girl. I now have a baby, and I hope he has the same kind of experience with someone like Monica. Every kid needs a Monica.

****

My kids brought her a skateboard once, and she rode it around our neighborhood. My kids tell that story to this very day.

****

Every year for about ten years, Monica put together the neighborhood Halloween party. She and Mike had no kids, but this was her party. It is definitely part of my kids' memories as they recall their childhood. We have many pictures of Monica holding the little ones year after year if they were scared of the costumes.

****

It is not Halloween without Monica's Halloween party.

****

Monica first thought of going to work in Omaha after college, but she said, "No, I have to go somewhere where it is warm. I can't be calling in to work because it is icy or snowy." That was good thinking on her part because she absolutely couldn't make it on ice at all. She said that when she was in college, they really helped her. She got a good job out there in California, and I can't say enough good things about her. Just because you are handicapped doesn't mean you can't do well. She has set a good example for the rest of us.

****

My kids loved her—it seemed that all kids loved her.

****

Monica—what can I say. The best description is that she never complained about her situation, never made any excuses, always seemed happy, and my kids always wanted to go to her house.

****

I met Monica when I was sixteen. My brother Mike brought her to my birthday party in the park. I noticed her missing limbs and the wheelchair and I thought, "Wow, that's different," but I was sixteen and it was my party so I was preoccupied. We did not see her again after this day. The next time I saw Monica was probably nine or ten years later when my brother announced he was moving in with her. I wondered if it was the same disabled girl from years before. I wondered how serious they were; however, my brother had been through a recent toxic marriage and divorce so maybe she was safe for him. Turns out, she was perfect for him. My brother always seems relaxed and happy with her. Monica is like any sister. Her disability has been an inconvenience with porch steps, but this just takes a little preplanning, a portable ramp, and a sense of humor. I love how she takes care of my brother. I am grateful for her "auntiness" to my children. I love her.

****

I met Monica sometime around 1981. She lived around the corner from me in Southern California. I had two kids at the time and I would sit on my cul-de-sac and watch them play. She had a friend who lived close to me, and she would pass by my house in her wheelchair going to visit her. She stopped once to say hello and meet my baby, and eventually we got to know each other. I was apprehensive of having a relationship with her. I had never been so friendly with someone before without legs and only one arm. I thought she would be so different and would not be able to do the same things I could. I didn't think we could possibly have anything in common. She was a bit of a mystery to me.

However, I enjoyed her company when she stopped briefly to chat, so I worked up the courage to ask her over for dinner. I remember being quite concerned about how the evening would go. What if she couldn't get in the front door? What if she had to go to the bathroom? Oh, what had I done? I prepared myself for one uncomfortable evening! My biggest worry was the table and chairs. Do I pull the chair away from the table so she can sit in her motorized wheelchair, or do I leave the chair as is and let her take care of herself? I didn't want to offend her.

Here comes the knock at the door. Monica asked if I would tip her chair back until the front wheels were on the step and then no problem—she's in! When the time came to eat, we had a brief discussion about seating arrangements, and she sat in my dining room chair, just like me.

That was the beginning of a long friendship that we still have today. As it turned out, we had a lot in common. Never again did I feel anxious around Monica, never again did I think I had to treat her differently. I had twins five years after I met her. She was working on one of her famous baby quilts before they were even conceived. Funny thing, the pattern on the blanket was that of a baby girl and boy and . . . that's what I had! She loved my kids and they loved her. I was very fortunate to have such a good friend by my side helping me raise my kids.

Over the years I witnessed on many occasions the general public treat Monica like a poor thing that either needed to be prayed for or be totally ignored (maybe she'll just go away). Kids would come up to her very innocently and ask her about her legs or arm, but most often their parent would rush up embarrassed and scold the child for talking to her. It was awkward and sad to see this ignorant behavior. Those of us who had the good fortune of having Monica in our lives have learned through her the importance of acceptance, diversity, and most of all, human kindness. Thanks, Monica, for teaching me and my children such valuable lessons!

CHAPTER 25

FINAL THOUGHTS

I believe in taking a positive attitude toward the world.
My hope still is to leave the world a little bit better than when I got here.
—Jim Henson

ALL IN ALL, I have a great life—no doubt greater than anyone expected or predicted. Many times I have wondered how my life would have turned out had a suitable "home" been found or had an ultrasound revealed my missing limbs prenatally.

Though naïve at first, I now realize that public biases toward me will always be present. For every new person I meet, I will encounter the same silent bias that is, ironically, quite natural. People will continue to ask me if I need help, and curious kids will be straightforward with questions. I once thought that if I had a life that mirrored a "normal" person, the preconceptions would go away, but I understand now that this will be an ongoing process with each new person I meet. Nonetheless, it is tiring and requires a lot of mental effort. Admittedly, there are times when I am simply tired of putting forth this effort.

Harder than this though is the effect of aging on a body with three missing limbs. Limitations increase, mobility decreases. My primary concern continues to be the protection of my arm. As the years pass, I have become more acutely aware of how close I am to needing a twenty-four-hour caregiver. I can't even process that stark reality. I am pretty sure, though, that I don't have enough determination, adaptation, or acceptance left in reserve if that were to happen.

Many things I could do easily before have become difficult, if not impossible now. I can no longer get on the floor or move quickly about (I remember playing baseball and how fast I could go). In order to transfer in and out of my chair, the height of both objects must be equal. I cannot pull myself back up. This immobility has been the most difficult truth of my life and is one that I never saw coming. I still do my best to focus on the things I can do and not on the things I can't do, but this is very hard. Mike and I had hoped to travel in our retirement years, but so far we have not figured out how we can do this.

On July 2, 2012, I went to my doctor's office for a routine checkup, and there was a new receptionist. When I asked her for a copy of a consult I had done, she said I needed to sign the "release of information" sheet. As she handed it to me, she stopped in midair and said loud enough for the crowded waiting room to hear, "Um . . . can you write?"

I am usually ready for such moments, but not this time. I was speechless. No one had ever asked me *that* before. I wondered, "Really? Did you just ask me if I could *write*—you mean like physically hold a pen?" The waiting room seemed eager for my answer as well. After a very pregnant pause, I slowly and deliberately said, "Yes . . . I can write."

While I was totally exasperated by the receptionist's question, I know that she probably thought she was being sensitive and kind, and she would have helped me had I said no. Based on my physical appearance alone, she really had no way to know whether I could write or not. I have to be careful not to take my years of frustration out on any one person, but frustrating it is.

Having a disability is simply a different way of life that no one, including me, would volunteer for. Parents would not volunteer to have a disabled child, yet after having one, most are surprised at how much this child taught them. Living disabled takes a lot more tolerance, ingenuity, creativity, fortitude, acceptance, and determination than living "normal." It requires an intense focus on things you can do and acceptance of those you cannot. It requires an understanding that people are inherently good and do not intend to insult you. It requires faith that there is a good reason for things in the big scheme of life.

Admittedly, I have wondered why I was chosen to be disabled. Why me? Grandma explained once that each of us is a single thread in God's big quilt and that the reason for the color of our thread will not be obvious until the entire quilt is finished.

My reason for writing this book was to keep a promise to my grandma. The more I wrote, the clearer the purpose for the book became, just as she said it would so many years ago. I do have an extraordinary life.

EPILOGUE

An error doesn't become a mistake until you refuse to correct it.
—Orlando Battista

ON AUGUST 31, 2012, the German pharmaceutical manufacturer of thalidomide, Chemie Grünenthal, made a worldwide public apology to the victims, families, and survivors for the devastating permanent effects of thalidomide. At the same time, they unveiled a bronze sculpture called "the Sick Child," which symbolizes the suffering of thalidomide babies born in the 1950s and 1960s. Many thought the apology was too little too late. Others saw it as a desperate plea for forgiveness.

Information continues to come forward, including the growing connection of thalidomide to the Nazi war camps. In its September 17, 2012, issue, *Newsweek* headlined an article entitled, "The Nazis at the Heart of the Worst Drug Scandal of All Time." It was subtitled, "Revelations of Their Connections with the Makers of a Deadly Drug."

Seeing this headline and reading the article unnerved me a little as I began to appreciate the possible magnitude of the thalidomide crisis and its cover-up. As I sit in my home today, it seems so far away, like it happened to someone else. Of course, however, it is painfully close, and it happened to me.

SERENITY PRAYER

God grant me the serenity
To accept the things I cannot change;
The courage to change the things I can;
And the wisdom to know the difference.

—Reinhold Niebuhr

Theresa (3) and me (7) in 1961.

Barbara, Theresa, Monica, Mike, 1961.

6 kids, David, Keith, Monica, Theresa, Barbara, Mike, December 1962.

Six kids with Dad, 1962.

　　MONICA SUCHA VICKERS

The boys' Christmas, 1963.

The girls' Christmas, 1963.

MONICA SUCHA VICKERS

Childhood home from 1958 to 1968.

My parents, Alvin and Agnes Sucha, February 1967.

INDEX

CPSIA information can be obtained at www.ICGtesting.com
Printed in the USA
BVOW02s0652311015

424531BV00003B/170/P